DID I REMEMBER TO TELL YOU?

A Real-Life Guidebook for Dementia Family Caregivers

PAM KOVACS JOHNSON

authorHOUSE

AuthorHouse™
1663 Liberty Drive
Bloomington, IN 47403
www.authorhouse.com
Phone: 833-262-8899

© 2020 Pam Kovacs Johnson. All rights reserved.

No part of this book may be reproduced, stored in a retrieval system, or transmitted by any means without the written permission of the author.

Published by AuthorHouse 08/31/2020

ISBN: 978-1-7283-7212-9 (sc)
ISBN: 978-1-7283-7211-2 (e)

Library of Congress Control Number: 2020916523

Print information available on the last page.

Any people depicted in stock imagery provided by Getty Images are models, and such images are being used for illustrative purposes only.
Certain stock imagery © Getty Images.

This book is printed on acid-free paper.

Because of the dynamic nature of the Internet, any web addresses or links contained in this book may have changed since publication and may no longer be valid. The views expressed in this work are solely those of the author and do not necessarily reflect the views of the publisher, and the publisher hereby disclaims any responsibility for them.

A Tree

Today a tree
Tomorrow a tree
But not the same
Except in name.

Each day
There is a change
For the tree
For me.

Contents

Dedication ix
A Word from the Author xi

Chapter 1   Everything Changes 1
Chapter 2   Dignity Matters 7
Chapter 3   Where Is There? 13
Chapter 4   A Heartfelt Apology 23
Chapter 5   The One and Only 29
Chapter 6   A Caregiver's Magical Mantra 37
Chapter 7   Listening with Our Hearts 45
Chapter 8   Are You Real Busy? 51
Chapter 9   Create an Illusion of Control 61
Chapter 10 Permission to Be Good Enough 67
Chapter 11 In Their Own Words 75
Chapter 12 A Life of Worthy Endeavors 83
Chapter 13 What If It Were So? 89
Chapter 14 Home is Where the Heart Is 99
Chapter 15 Superheroes 105
Chapter 16 Me Tarzan. You Jane. 115
Chapter 17 Sweet Secrets for Success 121
Chapter 18 You Can't Understand What You Don't Know 131
Chapter 19 Monsters After Midnight 139
Chapter 20 If They Can Walk, They Can Wander 147
Chapter 21 How About a Drink? 155

Chapter 22 The Power of Praise and Compliments......................161
Chapter 23 Grateful Hearts and Happy Souls...........................167
Chapter 24 When We Know Better 173

Acknowledgments 183
About the Author 185

Dedication

Charley Able
September 14, 1925 – January 1, 2020

This book is dedicated in loving memory to my dad - a great storyteller and a wonderful father. My dad loved to make people laugh and share entertaining stories of his youth. He cherished his family and his friends. Throughout my life with his words and examples, he showed me the importance of being kind, caring, and respectful.

A Word from the Author

This book is written especially for family members and special friends who are loving and caring for someone with Alzheimer's or another dementia. It is intended to be an easy-to-read, non-clinical guidebook to give families a real-life understanding of Alzheimer's and other forms of dementia. You will find it filled with ideas, approaches, and best practices for effective and compassionate dementia care, along with a bit of humor. My hope is that this book will help in making this difficult journey a little easier for you, the caregiver, as well as those living with any of these progressive neurological diseases.

I was first introduced to the disease as a pre-teen when my grandparents came to spend the summer with my family. This was in the early sixties before anyone knew the word "Alzheimer's." My paternal grandfather did and said a lot of crazy things during those months, and I learned a lot of new words that I had never heard before, certainly not ones that were used in our home. It was the first time I ever saw my grandmother cry. I think these were the roots of my lifelong passion to help families affected by this devastating illness.

For decades, it has been my honor and privilege to care for people in various stages of dementia and to provide support for their families. As a health care professional with extensive Alzheimer's knowledge, training, and more than 40 years in the field of aging, I really thought I had a good grasp of this disease as well as its impact on families. I was so wrong.

In 2008, my father came to live with me after my mother died. Having no siblings, I became his primary caregiver. Shortly thereafter, Dad was diagnosed with "mixed dementia," meaning he had both Alzheimer's Disease and Vascular Dementia. That was when my understanding of this disease came full circle, giving me an unimaginable viewpoint.

After years of urging and encouragement from family caregivers, I finally decided to write this book. My perspective has always been a bit unique in that I look at dementia care differently, with more of a what-if-it-were-me approach mixed with a bit of common sense. Now with a personal understanding of the disease I realize why it is so difficult for us, family caregivers, to do and say the right things. I have a renewed appreciation for the many challenges and emotions that become a routine part of each day.

This book gives practical information about dementia in a way that will allow you to understand exactly how the symptoms impact our loved-one and affect his or her abilities. It explains not only why we must say, do and respond differently than we did in our life before the disease, but tells you how to do it more effectively and compassionately.

In support of this project, many families have shared with me their own personal stories and experiences presuming that this might be of value to others. Some of these might even sound like yours, as many caregivers have had similar stories regardless of how one-of-a-kind they may seem. The names have been changed and the details are to the best of my recollection, but I would guess that some of my memories could be a convergence of different caregiver's narratives or situations.

You will read about their successful moments and mishaps as well as many of my own triumphs and mistakes. Although dementia is not a one size fits all, there are simply some approaches that work and those that do not.

Alzheimer's and other dementias are difficult and complicated diseases, and the keys to good care practices and techniques will be intertwined throughout various chapters. It is easy to be overwhelmed by the demands of caring for a loved one with dementia and there are countless things we need to hear more than once and in more than one way —again —and again.

Most of the content of this book addresses concerns, issues and challenges often encountered in the middle stages. For ease in both writing the book as well as for you the reader, I will frequently be using the term "dementia" throughout the book rather than just using the word "Alzheimer's." Although Alzheimer's disease is the most common cause of dementia, any type of dementia is physically, emotionally, and financially devastating. Also, I have predominately used the word "dementia" out of respect for families that are struggling to learn more as they are caring for loved-ones with other specific types, such as Lewy Body dementia (LBD), vascular cognitive impairment, Frontotemporal dementia (FTD), or Parkinson's dementia.

While I would suggest that the book be read from front to back as each chapter's content relates in some way to another, I hope that you will read it in the manner that best suits your personal needs and concerns. I encourage you to highlight and make notes in the margins to enable you to return to the book on those most demanding and trying days. I sincerely hope that you will find something in this book that is useful, along with a good reason to laugh or smile.

With gratitude,
Pam Johnson

Chapter 1

Everything Changes

At the time it seemed like a good idea. We were spending the day at the lake with our best friends, picnicking in a small secluded cove. When our husbands agreed to watch all four kids, my girlfriend and I decided it was finally our time to relax and have some fun. The two of us could barely fit in the children's inflatable boat, and the fact that it was round didn't help the situation. Somehow, each with a paddle in hand, we figured out how to stop going in circles and maneuvered the vessel away from shore. It was a genuine Goldilocks moment —not too hot, not to windy, even the waves were just right.

Briefly relieved of our parental responsibilities, it was easy to lose track of time. I'm not sure how long it was before we realized that we were no longer within the safe confines of the cove. While we were busy talking and soaking up the sun, the current had taken us out into the main body of the lake amongst a heavy barrage of fast boats and skiers. Looking back to shore, we could see the guys frantically yelling and waving, and the children hysterically watching. Although we couldn't hear any of them, we could see the panic on their faces. We were getting pretty scared too. This part of the adventure had not been in our plans.

We had been warned not to go too far. When our husbands started shouting commands to us from the shoreline, we had chosen to ignore their words of caution. We thought we knew better and would be just fine.

This is a true story that reminds me of my life as an Alzheimer's caregiver. Crazy as it might seem, there are many similarities. In the beginning, caring for a loved one with dementia is a good idea and seemingly the right thing to do. It is certainly something we think we can handle on our own. Even though we don't really know what we're doing, we still tend to figure it out the best we can, and then persevere. If we stop paying attention for just a minute, something can happen. When we take the time to look up from our situation, we discover that concerned family members and friends are anxiously waiting on the sidelines, willing to help. There are solutions to almost every problem. Sometimes it's as simple as taking a deep breath, remaining calm, and having a trusted person by our side to get us back safely onto solid ground. It can be both fun and frightening, but worth the risk.

As far back as I can remember, I learned great things from my father. He taught me words of wisdom, valuable life lessons, and how to be a good person. Now, I have learned from him about life with Alzheimer's in a way that has given me a deeper, more personal awareness.

Throughout my extensive career in long term care, I have enjoyed the challenges of serving people affected by such a complex and difficult disease. I have worked with countless individuals living in nursing homes and memory care units, most of whom were in the later stages of dementia.

In 2005, I opened Friends Place Adult Day Services, a specialized Alzheimer's adult day activity and health center. With only a few exceptions, all the members still live at home with their families and tend to be high functioning, in the middle stage of the disease. Typically, the majority are physically active. Due to the diverse ages of our staff, there have been a couple of times that it was hard to distinguish staff from client members. The ages of those diagnosed with Alzheimer's or another dementia have varied from forty-one years old to over one hundred.

This experience has also given me the opportunity to personally listen and learn more about the other side of this disease. Our members are often aware of their specific diagnoses. Sometimes they talk very openly about their feelings, happenings at home, worries about the family member caring for them, and a host of other concerns. As a specialized center, this environment sets the perfect stage for members to talk freely and openly, often sharing their thoughts and feelings with other members. Conversations and comments are unencumbered by any fears of saying the wrong thing or losing their train of thought. It's a powerful social peer group that functions almost like an informal support group at times.

For me professionally, it was always easy to do and say the right things. At least it was effortless, until the day I became my Dad's caregiver. How different it is when you are caring for other people's family members. You know them only in that moment of their life. There is no past, no family dynamics, no buttons that can be pushed. There is just today. Then, at the end of the day you go home. It's no wonder that it seemed so easy.

For some weird reason, when you are caring for your own family member, you tend to forget every single thing you know about this disease. I certainly did. During the first year that my dad was living with me, we both learned a lot of new things about the effect of this disease on memory, thinking and behavior. I also gained a much deeper understanding of many of the symptoms.

We were both surprised when there was an electrical fire in the lamp next to his bed. I was shocked that he would replace a 60-watt bulb with a 200-watt. He was astounded that it caused a problem. To him it just seemed to be the right thing to do if you wanted more light.

The time we encountered each other in the hallway between our bedrooms in the middle of the night, we were both a bit flabbergasted.

Since it was 1:30 a.m., he wondered what I was doing up so late. I couldn't begin to imagine why he was coming back from the garage with an electric drill in his hands. Dad explained that the hole in his new paper wall calendar was too small to go over the nail, so he had decided to use the drill to make a larger hole. As you might guess, I was not in agreement.

I still shudder to think about all the things that happened during those first few years that I never even knew about. It was only when my son slipped up and mentioned that Dad and his girlfriend got locked out of her house that I learned about one of his escapades. As a final desperate measure, he had called my son for help after unsuccessful attempts to find an unlocked window on the back side of the house. Only after swearing my son to secrecy did Dad confide all the details. At that time, he was in good physical shape and spry. He had stacked one of the aluminum garbage cans on top of the 96 gallon two-wheeled plastic trash can, climbed on top, then up and over the privacy fence. You can only imagine how upset I was. But he was amused by it all. And then things got worse when he tried to explain his way out of the situation by telling me it really wasn't a big deal. "Running and jumping up on the fence to climb back out of the yard…now, that was the real hard part!" he said, "I was afraid I might fall into the swimming pool."

Until it is in your home and you wake up every morning, go to sleep every night and worry about the tomorrows each day, you can't fully comprehend the impact of this disease. From the very first day you hear the diagnosis, your world, and theirs, begins to change. Shortly thereafter you realize that everything changes, again, and again. And so, must we.

Many of the changes with this disease occur ever so slowly and in such a subtle way that we often don't even realize when it's time to readjust, make modifications, or do things differently. We become acclimated to living in an unpredictable environment. We think we're fine, until the moment we finally realize that we are not. And, we also tend to think our loved-one is okay, and all is well –until something unexpected occurs.

It's like boiling a frog in water. According to the story, if a frog is placed in cold water on the stove, it senses no danger or reason to hop out. As the water slowly heats up, the frog gradually adjusts. By the time the water begins to boil, it's already too late. I don't know this for a fact and have wondered if anyone ever really boiled a frog, but it is a great little anecdote and illustrates my point.

All of us wish that our parent, spouse, friend, or partner had come with a book –like a personal instructional manual specifically about them. Perhaps then, we could be better equipped to anticipate what was going to happen next. Adjustments could be made, plans put into place, and time allocated for us to mentally prepare. We could expect the unexpected.

It would be even better if the manual had a special section in the back for troubleshooting. Imagine if we could look up any problem in the index, turn to the exact page, and find precisely the right answer. Now that would be a valuable resource book for caregivers to have handy!

> "Just when the caterpillar thought the world was over,
> it became a butterfly."
>
> – **Chuang Tzu (Zhuanzi)**

Chapter 2

Dignity Matters

Most people would not consider that the task of taking out the garbage is an important activity for maintaining someone's dignity. I certainly didn't, which was one of my first big mistakes after my father came to live with me. Every night after dinner, he insisted on emptying the kitchen trash. It didn't matter if it was full or nearly empty, out it went.

While I appreciated his wanting to help, it seemed ridiculous when we were often throwing away garbage bags with almost nothing in them. I just felt as if this was a huge waste of time and money. It was such a frustration that I finally calculated the cost of each of these trash liners. Dad had been frugal all his life so I knew he would be shocked to discover that this was costing us almost 12 cents a day. Then, it hit me how truly absurd I was being about all of this.

For as long as I could remember, this had always been Dad's job at home, and his regular nightly ritual. Thank goodness, I realized that this wasn't about removing garbage. It was about maintaining his dignity. What a small amount to pay for something so priceless! This responsibility gave him the opportunity to make a daily contribution, to feel useful and to maintain a sense of personal pride.

As a caregiver, it is easy to get caught up in little insignificant events and suddenly lose sight of what really matters most. Dignity is important to all of us. It is a common belief that each of us has an innate right to be valued as a human being and to be treated with dignity, always and everywhere. There should be no exceptions; and all people, with or without a disease, deserve to live their lives with dignity.

When we are children, good parenting techniques help us develop feelings of self-respect and positive self-esteem. Although a child usually doesn't understand or maybe even know the word dignity, they do know that they want to be seen and heard, feel safe and loved, and be treated nicely and fairly. And, from a very young age they want to be independent and do things *their* way.

As adults, we have those same intrinsic needs and desires. For our psychological well-being, it is essential that we feel safe and secure, loved, and accepted, respected by others, and maintain a sense of independence. For someone with cognitive impairment, it takes the supportive and intentional efforts of a valuable caregiver to preserve these affirmative feelings of self-worth and dignity.

Although we have set goals personally and professionally throughout our lives, families seldom think about having a definitive caregiving goal. All our goals serve to define what we hope and plan to accomplish in any given situation of our life. It makes us think about doing things in a very specific way to achieve a desired outcome.

Dementia does not change one's need or desire to continue to lead an active, productive life or to be treated with honor and respect. Keeping "dignity" foremost in our hearts and minds as our overall goal of care, enables us to care for our loved ones in a manner that instills feelings of worthiness and admiration. With this objective, the symptoms of dementia can be managed for many years and in ways that enable people to stay independent longer, function better, and maintain an acceptable quality of life.

Ultimately to achieve this desired goal of care, we need to change the way we think, act, and speak or we will not be successful. We must start doing everything differently than we did for many years before this disease entered our lives. Our old ways will no longer work. Certainly not in a way that provides a compassionate type of care. Developing new habits, scripting conversations, readying our responses, and being consciously aware of opportunities to help our loved ones maintain their dignity are truly in everyone's best interest.

I learned the hard way how difficult and hurtful it can be when we don't pay attention and let go of some of our old habits. During our lifetimes we become accustomed to saying certain things to others out of habit, without even thinking about the impact these same words might have on someone with memory problems. It's during those times when we ask questions or make comments that are thoughtless and do not reflect our love, dignity, or respect.

It wasn't until one day in the car when my dad and I were talking, that I realized I kept making the same mistake over and over. It was a serious, inexcusable blunder on my part. As I was driving, we were discussing our dinner plans. This same conversation had started that morning and continued throughout the day. (Many, many times throughout the day.) Slightly in my own defense, I might add that this was at a time when my dad was in the early stage of dementia and still able to remember his diagnosis, his personal social plans, or any details or events involving his girlfriend. Seldom did it seem that he was able to recall things that mattered to me.

My dad said to me, "So, did you decide where you'd like to go for dinner?"

"Dad!" I said, "Don't you remember? We're having dinner at the kid's house."

He turned, glanced out the window, and after a few seconds my normally, happy-go-lucky dad looked at me and said in a sad but deliberate tone, "Don't *you* remember...I have Alzheimer's!"

I swallowed hard all the while wondering how I could have been so terribly insensitive. His sincere response definitely put everything back into a proper perspective for both of us. I knew better than to ask someone with memory problems if they remembered something.

And I would never do that with anyone else with dementia I knew or cared for. For me, it was always very clear and logical that when one remembers, they don't ask us the questions. I was also aware that because of the vascular dementia, his ability to recall detailed information fluctuated and many days was based more on luck than personal choice.

I'm pretty sure that was the last time I asked him such a senseless and dreadful question. Unfortunately, it was not the first time. Anytime those words slipped out of my mouth, my heart filled with deep regrets. Like most caregivers there is an unwarranted struggle with being able consistently to recall that they have a memory problem. Countless times before when I would catch myself speaking without thinking, I would end up almost shaking or pounding on the desk or steering wheel out of frustration saying, "Why can't I remember that he… can't… remember!"

But it was on that grievous day when I realized that I had to do something different in order to stop myself once and for all. I had to find a better way and kinder words to use when I was with him and no longer be tempted to reply the way I often do with other people in my life. Knowing that old habits are hard to break, I decided that from then on, I needed to have a consistent scripted, caring response. After that I no longer posed that old awful question - either literally or rhetorically. Instead, I adopted a positive practiced pattern of beginning most of our conversations with this straightforward yes or no question. "Did I remember to tell you…?"

There are many simple ways for us to care for a loved-one in a manner that instills feelings of love, respect, and admiration.

- Praise frequently and sincerely.
- Value each person as a unique individual.
- Express gratitude.
- Offer choices and solicit their opinions.
- Focus on their strengths and remaining abilities.

- Be mindful of the person's lifetime roles.
- Allow them to help.
- Communicate respectfully.
- Promote independence.
- Listen with your heart.
- Recognize your limitations.
- Accept their limitations.
- Stay socially connected.
- Laugh together.

Best dementia care practices go way beyond ensuring that a person's basic needs are being met. It's an approach that strives to achieve and/or maintain an optimal level of physical, intellectual, and emotional wellness. Each of us want to live our lives in a way that allows us to socialize, actively participate, contribute, and enjoy a life with meaning and purpose…a life with dignity.

These techniques and approaches are not going to make everything perfect and wonderful. But they can make life better and easier because this model of dementia care will ease many of the day-to-day challenges and frustrations. Use them as guidelines for developing new habits of doing and saying things so that at the end of each day, both of you still have your self-esteem intact. Then you'll likely discover renewed feelings of personal pleasure and accomplishment each time you successfully rekindle their sense of dignity.

Years ago, when I was a manager at a nursing home, I became acquainted with an elderly and well-respected, retired professor. He was a charismatic, lifelong bachelor, who had traveled extensively, and lectured at colleges and universities around the world. Throughout his life he became accustomed to staying in hotels, often for long periods of time. So, when he moved into the memory care community, he often perceived it as merely another hotel. When he would get restless, he would occasionally go to the nurse's station requesting them to prepare his bill so that he could settle his account and be on his way. One day he was demanding the "waitress" (one of the nurse's aides) bring him his ticket so that he could pay for his lunch before he left. I happened to be in the dining room, so I went to his table, turned over the paper dietary menu on his tray, and suggested he sign the back. Then I informed him we would be glad to "charge it to his room." That pleased him and became our normal protocol for him at mealtimes.

Then one evening after he had leisurely charmed his way through dinner while enjoying the company of three ladies, he summoned one of the nursing staff. "Waitress, waitress," he called as he motioned in the air with his hand for her to come over to his table. Leaning back in his chair, swelled with pride and elation he announced, "Bring me all their tickets. Dinner is on me tonight!" Without missing a beat, she stopped what she was doing, gathered up the menus from each of the women's trays; and, with a polite smile, handed them to him along with a pen. This story illustrates how easy it can be to show indisputable respect for people living with dementia and enable them to maintain their dignity. And for two individuals to feel proud.

Every time we do or say anything using best dementia care practices, we are in fact caring for them in a way that allows us to give them a loving gift. After all, gifts are something given freely without the expectation of anything in return. Our actions, words and deeds become gestures of our affection. These are little acts of kindness that breathe personal pride back into their life…and yours.

> **"The greatest virtues are those which are most useful to other persons."**
> — **Aristotle**

Chapter 3

Where Is There?

We had been on the phone for almost an hour when he said, "It sounds like everything I've been saying to my wife has been wrong." I could clearly hear the sadness and disappointment in his voice. As gently as I could, I explained, "It's not wrong. It's just that those words don't work anymore."

For the past few years, since his wife was diagnosed with Alzheimer's, they had both managed just fine. Her short-term memory loss had created some inconveniences at times, but they had adjusted. Now nothing seemed to be going right at home. Jonathon shared that they "couldn't talk to each other" anymore. When he said something to Anne, he felt as if she either ignored him or defied him. And he said that about half the time he had no idea what she was trying to tell him. "But mostly," he added, "she doesn't say much of anything. She just looks at me."

Language is incredibly important in all our lives. We use our words and body language to state our needs and desires, share our thoughts and opinions, express our feelings and emotions, and maintain social relationships.

When dementia moves into our homes and impairs the language skills of our loved ones, it creates enormous challenges for everyone. At some time during our lives and relationships with our loved ones, before the dementia, we have probably dealt with their forgetting something, exercising poor judgment, making a bad decision, or acting in a way we found annoying or upsetting. In the past whenever there might have been conflicts or personal differences resulting in a breakdown in communication, at least we could still converse. Even if some of our words were not loving or effectively persuasive, we used a common language.

Before this disease, each of us was still capable of intentional speech and could understand the words spoken by the other. But now, for all practical purposes, we find we no longer speak the same "language." At least not in the same way we did before nor in the typical manner that we are accustomed to using with others in our daily lives. For several decades, I have encouraged family caregivers to consider thinking in terms of adopting a new language —a "Language of Dignity"— to help them remember to speak and word things differently.

The simple idea behind this jargon is the premise that dignity, love, acceptance, and respect all comprise a universal language, understood by all, used with or without words. It seems only logical for this also to be the perfect universal language for dementia care.

Good, effective, and compassionate communication creates the sturdy foundation on which caregivers can build all other needed dementia care skills. Our words, when chosen carefully, allow us to stay socially connected, can help minimize or prevent many of the disease-related behaviors, and enable us to assist with their activities of daily living with little or no drama.

The loss of language skills doesn't happen overnight. It happens gradually, a few words at a time. Usually it begins with difficulty with word finding – remembering specific names of familiar people, places, or things. When we're not paying close attention to what is really happening, it certainly can seem as though it has happened overnight. Seldom are we properly prepared for that day when we suddenly realize that our conversations have become cryptic in nature.

The missing nouns or misused words cause each sentence to become like a puzzle that must be solved before we can respond or even comment. I believe that is how our "messages" are received by our loved ones as well. Lots of missing words creating many confusing sentences.

Many caregivers have learned the hard way that most questions should be avoided, completely inaccurate answers will be given, and meaningful conversations are far and few between. We think we are speaking in a clear and easy-to-understand way. Perhaps it is apparent to others, those people not encumbered by language deficits. Often, without a thought, we use ambiguous words that are confusing to them and ask too many foolish questions, only to be surprised or disappointed by the outcomes.

My all-time favorite story details what happened when a friend of mine took her mother to the emergency room at a local hospital. Sandy completely understood her mother's limitations and the absurdity of asking questions. When the nurse came into the room, Sandy informed her that her mother, Hazel, had late mid-stage Alzheimer's. Without even the slightest hint of acknowledgement, the nurse immediately began asking her mother questions from the mini-mental status exam. Hazel sat on the side of the exam table, uncomfortably quiet and confused.

Sandy pulled the nurse aside, once again explaining, "My mom has severe dementia."

"I know!" said the nurse. Then turned to ask Hazel, "Can you tell me what the date is?"

"Yes," she said.

"Uh…so… what day is this?" the nurse asked.

"You don't know?" Hazel replied looking somewhat bewildered that the nurse was asking something so nonsensical. Then looking over at Sandy, smiled and just shrugged her shoulders.

"Can you tell me where you are?" asked the nurse as she moved on to the next question.

Hazel leaned forward towards the nurse with her eyes squinted and looking somewhat baffled. She shrugged her shoulders once again but said nothing.

"Where… are… you… now?" the nurse carefully enunciated in a slightly louder voice.

"I'm …Right…Here!" Hazel boldly responded.

I have no doubts that the nurse thought she was being perfectly clear, and the questions were all straightforward. And I would guess by Hazel's responses and demeaner that she felt like those were some pretty silly questions. Besides the fact that this is a funny story and entirely true, it illustrates other noteworthy points. It is a stark reminder that people with dementia are forgetful, often disoriented, but not stupid. The narrative demonstrates that when our loved ones hear our words, they will give a somewhat appropriate response according to their interpretation and understanding of the question. This means a correct answer is not always going to be the one we're expecting. Dementia fills our lives with day-to-day surprises and snippets of humor.

If anyone has ever had a word stuck on the tip of their tongue or forgotten a dear friend's name in the middle of an introduction, they can relate to the accompanying feelings of embarrassment and frustration. Imagine that happening all day…every day! With dementia, what first appears as a difficulty with a few words, usually nouns, then progresses into an awkwardness or inability to express full thoughts or ideas. Because of this they become reluctant to initiate conversations and tend to withdraw socially. They have enough awareness to know that there are certain things that they *should* know and questions that they *should* be able to answer.

When caregivers speak in a language of dignity, we do not ask "stupid" questions. While there's a common belief, and it is often said that there is no such thing as a stupid question, in dementia care just about any **open-ended question** is most likely going to seem pretty stupid. And for anyone living with dementia (especially in the middle stages), these kinds of questions are neither caring nor considerate. These questions only serve to showcase our loved one's shortcomings, and yield nothing but negative, unpleasant outcomes.

Caregivers need to realize that sometimes "yes" is just a word. It's not necessarily an answer. Rather, it's just a quick and easy reply to a question they don't understand well enough to answer accurately. This is also true of other common responses that families often hear, such as "No," "I don't know," or "It doesn't matter."

With dementia, there is an awareness of being asked, but an inability to fully comprehend or process enough of the words to provide an honest, straightforward reply. This often causes them to respond too quickly or make a "best guess" at what they think might be a favorable response.

On several occasions, I would hear my dad talking to other people and agreeing to things I knew he didn't like. One day when this happened, I finally asked him if he understood their question. "Not really," he said. "So, why would you say yes?" I asked. "I don't know," he said matter-of-factly, "I thought maybe it was the right answer."

As caregivers we have heard those words, "I don't know," all too many times. Practically any time we mistakenly ask our loved one any question beginning with Who, What, Where, When, or Why, we can rest assured that "I don't know" will most likely be the response. But for our loved ones it is rarely a cheerful response. Instead we will hear this reply with tones of sadness, disappointment, or embarrassment, regardless of how trivial the question may be. We don't want them feeling these negative emotions and certainly don't want to be the cause. But there comes a time in this disease when just about any question will seem as though we are challenging their intelligence – testing them. And with dementia, testing is always going to be stressful.

Using the principles of this new "language of dignity" filled with positive words and an encouraging tone of voice, we can pose comments in a way that allows our loved ones to successfully respond or gently guides them to the answer with cues or prompts. We can remember for them and kindly give them a socially acceptable reason for being unable to recall. At the same time, we are observing our loved one's body language, so we know when to provide them with additional information or just move on to something else.

We don't ask **who**, because saying "Who is the girl in this picture?" can be stressful. Instead we use a dialogue which might help them to recall or politely grants permission to have forgotten. "I think this is a photograph of your beautiful great granddaughter Alyssa. You probably don't remember her. It's been a long time since you have seen her." This will likely yield a far better reaction as you have expressed a thoughtful comment which might also be a pleasant conversation starter.

We don't ask **what** questions. It doesn't matter if we are trying to find out about what happened or determine a loved one's personal preference, because this will seldom lead us to the answer. If we make the mistake of asking, rather than receiving an answer, they will just give us back the question. This is frustrating when we are trying to determine our loved one's personal preference, opinion or need. Instead of a candid response, one might hear, "What do *you* want me to wear?" "What do *you* want me to do?" Responding back to them with an "I don't care," is not going to be helpful either. When this happens, try asking as a **closed question**, posing the answer for them, then ask for their agreement. "Would you like to wear this blue plaid shirt today?" "Let's watch TV. Does that sound good?" "I think it would be nice to go for a walk together. Would you enjoy that?"

We don't ask, "**What** do you want to eat?" This is a common dilemma when families dine away from home. More often than not, this question is answered with "I'll have whatever you're having." Other times we might even hear, "I'm not really hungry," or "I don't know." At many of the popular restaurants, the menu selections can be overwhelming even for one without cognitive impairments. Our loved ones need us to give them some direction. It is seldom that they don't know what they like to eat or would want to order. They can't make decisions when they don't know the options. Typically, they either don't recognize the menu selections —the names or the items— or they can't find the right words to express personally or identify their preference. Consistently patronizing only a few restaurants where our loved one has one or two favorite menu items can make this a more satisfying dining experience for everyone. Simple and familiar will always yield the best results.

Not too long ago I was watching an old classic movie in which an elegant, unattached couple were dining in a posh restaurant. She seemed a little out of her element and was obviously uncomfortable gazing at the extravagant menu. But he, being the perfect gentlemen, politely asked, "My dear, may I have the pleasure of ordering for you tonight?" It was wonderfully romantic. Later, as I reflected on that scene, I realized what a great line it would be for us to use when we are dining with our loved-one and wish to relieve them of the ordeal of selecting their own meal.

We don't ask **what** happened when we see a new bruise, scratch, or small injury. It's easy to make this mistake when dealing with minor medical mysteries associated with dementia. Upon discovery, a polite more effective remark might be, "You have a bruise on your arm". It's now a casual, caring comment, no longer a query. Then if our loved one has even the slightest clue as to what happened, he or she will likely volunteer an explanation. If not, move on. I've seen many a time when the family pushes too hard for an answer and instead they receive a fabricated response. Or they might hear a convoluted memory of something that may well have occurred many years ago.

Our loved one is not intentionally lying but is voicing a seemingly logical explanation as though it was a fact. "I fell." "Someone hit me." That doesn't always mean that it is the truth. When my dad was living in memory care, the first (and only time) I asked him about a bruise on his forehead, he said "that guy" hit him. Before I could foolishly ask anything else, he added, "So I punched him back and knocked him across the room!" Later the staff clarified that there had not been a boxing match in the dining room, but rather Dad had bumped his head on the bathroom door. However, there are times when we need to further investigate and try to discover what really might have happened so as better to understand and prevent future occurrences. This is a much bigger concern when there are others assisting with the care of our loved one, either in our home or a community care setting.

Most of the time we can probably make a good, educated guess as to how it happened. Due to increasing problems with depth perception caused by the dementia, coupled with thinning skin due to aging, small bruises or little cuts on the arms and hips will be seen more often. They will bump into the corners of doors, cabinets, and furniture much more frequently.

We don't ask **when.** To ask any question beginning with the word "when," is not only unwise but is totally ridiculous. Rarely do people with mid-stage dementia have any awareness of time. For them, the concept of time is both complicated and elusive. There is no clear understanding of the measure of time, be it minutes, hours, days, weeks, or months. Numbers become merely abstract words with no actual meaning or relevance. Days are just "days' with no sense of order or meaning. The past and present are vague, at times completely entwined. In their world events have happened now, before now or some other time.

So maybe the next time you tell your loved one that we're not leaving the house for another hour and they keep coming back every five minutes, you might understand why. This might also help explain why it is that when you say, "I'll be right back," they can become anxious during your brief absence. To them it seemed as if you were away for hours!

We don't ask **where.** Just guessing, I would estimate that at least a million times, I've heard caregivers ask, "Where is your walker?" Really? I mean think about that question. We're asking someone with a serious memory problem to tell us where they have left their walker. Do they even know they have a walker? Do they have the slightest clue to why they are supposed to be using this thing? I sincerely doubt our loved ones intentionally walk around without them just to make us crazy. (Although in the past that thought might have entered my mind a few times.) Most of our loved ones don't think they need it or remember why they even got it in the first place. Some of them have not the foggiest idea that this contraption even belongs to them.

Rather than asking **where** your loved one's purse, wallet, keys, walker, or anything else is, willingly assume that they don't know either. If you press them on the location, they will tell you emphatically where they put the item or the place where it "always is." In their mind that is where it should be. So, when it's not "there," the only logical explanation to them is that someone else either moved it or took it. Begin by stating something kind and empathetic. "I misplace my stuff all the time, too." "Isn't it frustrating when we can't find something?" "Can I help you look for it?" "Maybe someone moved it." "I wonder if someone might have borrowed it?" "I'll be glad to try to help you find it."

And, most importantly, we don't ask **why.** "Why did you do that?" "Why did you say that?" These are definitely the kinds of questions which caregivers unwittingly ask too often. Deep in our heart, we all know and can appreciate that any question beginning with the word "why" is going to be far too complicated. Surely, as caregivers, we know better than to think that we would ever be able to get an accurate response. Without any misgivings, we fully realize it will always be the same answer. "I don't know." This response should never surprise us, because for them, this is the only truthful, honest, and correct reply to an unanswerable question.

So why do we keep asking these questions? It's another one of those times when caregivers might stop and wonder, which one of us has impaired judgment, thinking and a memory problem. I know for a fact that since I became a family caregiver, I have questioned my own mental status on more than one occasion. One reason might be that old habits are hard to break but that is never a good excuse. Changes are tough but learning to communicate differently is undeniably worth the effort.

To be the kind of caregiver whom most of us want to be, we need to follow a dementia code of conduct, practice using a language of dignity and strive to speak compassionately. Being able to effectively communicate is essential to an individual's sense of well-being and vital in our role as caregivers. But it's never easy and takes a great deal of practice, patience… and more practice.

> **"A person hears only what they understand."**
> **— Johann Wolfgang von Goethe**

Chapter 4

A Heartfelt Apology

An apology can strengthen and improve almost any relationship in nearly every situation, especially in dementia care. For caregivers, saying, "I'm sorry" to our loved ones are powerful words. Almost magically, these two little words can end an argument, prevent a catastrophic incident, or exemplify empathy. When we sincerely apologize, it doesn't mean it is our fault or indicate it has anything to do with us personally. It simply means we care and acknowledges our understanding. It's amazing how quickly we can learn not to argue, deny, or explain, but merely ask for forgiveness. When we use a what-if-it-were-me approach, we begin to view situations through the eyes and hearts of our loved ones, and our apology often follows as a natural reaction to their thoughts and feelings. Sometimes we need to be guided to this conclusion.

Gloria was a loving daughter and caregiver. She had called the center several times within thirty minutes pleading for some guidance. "I hadn't even had my first cup of coffee before Mama came into the kitchen screaming at me and saying she knew I had stolen all of her money," Gloria was explaining to a staff member on the phone. By now she was at her wit's end and her mother was still livid, as both of them had been arguing for almost two straight hours.

Before I reached my office, the staff had offered Gloria several different suggestions to help convince her mother that she would never steal anything and reassure her that all of her money was still secure. Within a few minutes of my arrival, the phone rang again. It was Gloria and even from the doorway, I could hear her mother's furious accusations in the background. I told her to take a deep breath, muster up all her love, and go apologize to her mother with the utmost sincerity. "But I didn't take her money!" she said tearfully. I quickly explained that right now only her mother's "truth" mattered. Unless she was willing to accept the blame, and promise to never "do it again," the arguments were likely to continue.

When two truths collide, only one will prevail. Although not one dollar had actually left her mother's account, together we came up with a plausible story about why she "took" the money (not stole it) thinking it would be wise to move some of it into another financial account, perhaps for better investment advantages. Also, Gloria understood and agreed to express substantial regret over not discussing this decision first with her mother. After a heartfelt apology to her mother, all was forgiven, and soon forgotten.

As this disease progresses, we all become convincing storytellers. It's how we survive the delusions and paranoid behaviors so common with dementia. This is partly because in the world of Alzheimer's or any form of dementia, nothing is ever misunderstood, lost, or misplaced. It's been stolen. Ask any seasoned caregiver and they'll quickly confirm that austere fact.

When an older friend of mine with Alzheimer's was living in an independent senior apartment complex, she was able to manage quite well until she started losing her keys. The keys were not nearly as much of a concern as the problems caused by her increasing anxiety over "those" people coming in and taking things. Nothing else ever seemed to be missing; and when the keys were occasionally located within her apartment, she would only become more enraged stating, "The damn thieves came in again and brought them back." All of this resulted in such mistrust that she refused to let the housekeepers clean her room, barricaded her door at night, and started hiding her jewelry and other personal items. She would continue to relocate her prized possessions over and over, seeking out a more secretive place each time. Eventually it became nearly impossible for her or anyone else to find any of the items that magically disappeared on a daily basis.

During that time, I remember telling her often how very sorry I was that she was having to deal with all these problems. I was sorry that someone had "stolen" her watch, lipstick, TV Guide, and favorite sweater. Frankly, I was most remorseful and sincerely sorry she was living so much of the time filled with fear for her personal safety and the security of her belongings.

I think of an apology as merely empathy in its purest form. One caregiver used it sincerely and skillfully each time she dealt with her husband's hallucinations. Rather than confirming or denying his hallucinatory visions, she chose instead to be guided by her heart. Although he frequently experienced people or animals which were not there, his visions were not as frightening as is usually common for someone with Lewy Body dementia. However, they were quite alarming to him. Since LBD is notorious for producing rollercoaster types of cognitive fluctuations, he was fully aware that his mind moved in and out of reality often leaving him unclear about what was real and what was not. He found this uncertainly to be both unsettling and sometimes embarrassing.

Just as many people might do when trying to keep a grip on uncontrollable circumstances, he tried to ignore it and pretend as though these sightings were not happening. At first when his guard was down and his wife noticed him obviously distracted by what he had noticed and was intently watching, she would ask him if he saw "something over there." Practically every time he would deny seeing anything but was clearly uncomfortable. Then she stopped asking "if" and instead accepted these visions as being real to him, regardless of the fact that he alone could see them. With great candor and compassion, she would apologize to him for her inability to witness and share in his visions. I can still hear her calm voice saying, "I'm so sorry that I can't see them. Tell me about them." She would ask questions about the kids, animals, or other details and patiently wait for his response as though it was a normal, everyday conversation any loving couple might have.

Seldom is there a day in the life of a caregiver in which we are not presented with an opportunity to express our regrets. We can be truly sorry that…

- you're having these memory problems.
- you have Alzheimer's (dementia, LBD, Parkinson's, FTD).
- the doctor says your showers must be supervised.
- I can't understand what you are wanting to tell me.
- you can't live in your own home.
- sometimes life is so confusing.
- you can't do all the things you used to do.
- all of this is so difficult.

As you already know, this list easily goes on.

Through the years with many others, including my dad, I often word things in a way that might imply that I am the one who no longer remembers. With them, I will candidly question the accuracy of my own memories. "I'm not sure I knew that," "I can't seem to remember when that was either," "I don't know for sure; names are pretty hard for me to remember."

Frequently, when Dad was miffed or caught off guard by someone or something of which he appeared to have no knowledge, I would often say, "I'm sorry, I must have forgotten to tell you." At times, I have also used it to shift the blame from someone else that had upset him and allow me to be the one at fault. He tended to forgive me (the favorite daughter) quicker than others. My dad had made his bed every single morning, without exception, for as long as I could remember. That was one thing that did not change when he moved into a memory care facility. It wasn't discussed with him or the staff at his new place. Since he was physically able and liked being independent, I assumed he would still want to continue with his routine morning task. So, every morning when the staff came into his room, they found his bed already made.

Then one day at lunch, he found out from the other men that none of them made their beds. The staff did that for them. By the time I got there that afternoon to visit with him, he was so mad, saying, "I pay my way just like the rest of them! Why does everybody else get their bed made but not me?" The conversation was much longer, and my attempt to explain was both brief and unacceptable to him. So, I did what I believed in my heart was the best thing I could do. I lied and apologized.

I told him that it was all my fault. Then, I went on to say that I was the one who told the staff not to come into his room to make his bed. "My dad can still make his own bed," I said to them, "and he doesn't need anyone to do that for him now". With a sincere and respectful tone, I added, "I'm so sorry that I didn't ask you. This should have been your decision not mine." Instantly, his anger dissolved. It was much easier for him to be displeased with staff members he barely knew rather than his own beloved daughter. Together we discussed the issue some more and I told him that I would be glad to tell the staff to please start making his bed each day. It seemed the only natural thing to do since I was now the one to blame.

Empathy is essential to our emotional wellness. Apologies acknowledge a person's feelings. Expressing remorse is easier and kinder than telling someone they are confused, wrong or have already been told countless times. For years after a 1970's movie, people were frequently talking about not having to say you are sorry when you love someone. Unlike the implication from that old movie, for us it's just the opposite. For caregivers when we love someone it means we're *always* having to say we're sorry. When those mighty words flow from the bottom of our hearts, a heartfelt apology shows our loved ones that we care enough to willingly accept the blame or acknowledge their sorrow.

> "An apology is the superglue of life. It can repair just about anything."
> — **Lynn Johnston**

- FOR BETTER OR FOR WORSE © 1994 Lynn Johnston Productions. Dist. By ANDREWS MCMEEL SYNDICATION. Reprinted with permission. All rights reserved.

Chapter 5

The One and Only

Not another person in the entire world is exactly like you or me. Each of us has our own talents, skills, likes, dislikes, and personalities. Some of our traits might change due to age, disease, or circumstances, but what always remains is an adult who is a distinctive individual deserving of respect. To value another, means that we show respect for their ideas and feelings, honor the complications in their lives, and accept their uniqueness.

Dementia makes a lot of things more complicated. People with this disease are still the same individuals and yet can appear to be quite dissimilar than they were previously. Often a family member does not see their loved one with the same heart and eyes as another member of the family might see them.

This was the case with Larry's wife and his son, Max. During the past few months, Max had been coming each afternoon to pick up his father from the respite program. One day he arrived earlier than usual in hopes of joining his dad for the weekly scheduled entertainment. "It's so great to see Dad laughing, dancing, and having fun," he said as he watched from the fringes of the music room. Then he added, "And he's smiling and happy all the way home. Wish I could figure out how to make my Mom happy."

With great sorrow Max explained that it seemed as though his mother was mad almost all of the time, either at his father or because of his father. During the past year Larry had been noticeably declining; he had lost most of his language skills and needed assistance with many of his activities of daily living. However, he could still smile and dance. His mother constantly complained that his dad —her husband— was being ridiculous, acting like a "silly child," and going about his day "without a care in the world." Max said he didn't understand why his mother couldn't just be glad that his dad was cheerful and content. His dad had worked hard, been both a good father and caring husband, and enjoyed spending time with friends and family throughout his entire life.

After many years of living with dementia, Larry was not the same "husband," although he remained kind and caring. Now, through no fault of his own, he truly didn't have a care in the world. But he was still having a good time. Whenever there was a live music event at the center, he was inevitably the first one up and out of his chair, onto the dance floor, every time without exception. Even when Christmas songs were played, he would jitterbug to "Jingle Bells" and Foxtrot to the solemn tune of "Silent Night."

When caregivers value a loved one as a unique individual, we also accept him or her just as he or she is now. As the disease progresses, our loved ones are going to change in many ways. We also need to change our expectation so that we can continue to accept and value them as the person they are at any given moment. On a daily basis, we have to remind ourselves that regardless of what they might say or do, they are doing the best they can…that day …at that time. It helps for us to remember that three of the most important words in dementia care are love, respect, and acceptance.

It's been decades but I still remember the two daughters who frequently came to visit their mother Millie at one of the nursing homes where I served as the Administrator. Their mom was in the late middle stage of Alzheimer's and quite different from the mother they knew before this tragic disease. Despite the dementia, she was delightfully happy all the time. Throughout the day she busied herself by going in and out of her room, changing her clothes numerous times. Sometimes when her daughters came, she might have had her shoes on the wrong feet, a top on backwards or her sweater inside out. It didn't bother her, and she loved bragging that she had dressed herself.

Carolyn, the youngest daughter didn't seem to mind or care either. During their visits she and her mom would often sit on the front porch "people watching," as they called it. They looked and listened to the birds singing, and watched the cars passing by. Their time together was filled with joy and laughter as they talked about everything and nothing. They simply relished just being in the moment together.

Unfortunately, Mary, the oldest daughter, took issue with her mother's not always being dressed properly and was disturbed by her occasional outrageous behavior. One day Millie jumped up in the middle of their visit. When she ran over and threw her arms around a strange man that had walked in the door, I honestly thought Mary was going to die of humiliation, right there on the spot. "Mother! Why would you do that?" she shouted. With the sweetest, most innocent voice her mother responded, "Why shouldn't I?"

On one occasion, both daughters came to visit on the same day at almost the same time. Carolyn and Millie were already out on the front porch sitting on the bench, so when Mary arrived, she went over and joined them. Mary had no sooner sat down when she started reprimanding her mother. "Mother, your shoes are on the wrong feet…again!" Millie suddenly turned from one daughter to the other looking equally bewildered, hurt, and sad, but said nothing.

In a flash, Carolyn took off both of her own shoes and put them back on the opposite feet. Then as she affectionately leaned against her mother, they both stretched out their legs in front of them with their feet together, toes pointing up and just started giggling. When Millie pointed her finger at Mary's shoes, she and Carolyn began laughing even louder. Suddenly, Mary was the different one.

Whenever I think back on that story, I am filled with sadness for Mary. She was so caught up in grieving the mother who was being taken away by Alzheimer's that she wasn't able to appreciate the "new" mother who was still alive and with her now. Mary had wasted a number of opportunities to create new memories with her mom.

Carolyn's perspective was very different from that of her sister's. She, too, missed the mother in whom she used to confide, ask for advice, share her personal triumphs, or bemoan life's disappointments. Because she loved "both" of her mothers, Carolyn had made up her mind that she would choose joy for today and save her grief for all of the tomorrows when her Mom would be gone forever.

Naturally, there are times when we are going to grieve during this journey. It seeps into our thoughts. But for today, let's stay focused on the present and value our loved ones despite any alterations in personality, appearance, or behavior which have occurred. While at times it can be disturbing because they might look or act differently, the person we love is still there …somewhere deep inside. They will remain our beloved spouse, parent, partner, or cherished friend long after everything else has changed.

When our loved one's decision-making process becomes limited, caregivers might start the conversations by sharing ***our*** opinions. Then, ask for their comments or a confirmation. Do they agree or disagree? A basic question, but nevertheless engaging. It really doesn't matter if we are discussing politics, or world affairs, or buying a new refrigerator. Just ask them. It reaffirms that what they think still matters. It will give them the chance to feel as if they still have some say in their daily lives, a sense of control, and your respect. As language skills become further impaired and word finding increasingly difficult, it is even more critical that we put forth every effort to ask. Even merely seeking out their approval will help preserve their personhood.

Our identity, the essence of each of us as a person, is often defined by our interests, experiences, views, and beliefs. It is who we are.

Solicit the thoughts and opinions of our loved ones. Ask them about the things that mattered to them, their former interests, or areas of expertise. Good results are likely to occur when we ask a mother about childrearing, an accountant about numbers, a homemaker about cooking, or a sportsman about hunting or fishing. I'm sure you get the idea.

Jeff often stopped by his parents' house after work. It gave his mom at least a little break from caregiving and afforded him some one-on-one time with his dad who suffered from vascular dementia. Just sitting and having conversations was challenging, so they would go for a walk around the neighborhood.

When Jeff was growing up, his father had been a serious car enthusiast, often quizzing the kids about the make and model of any vehicle they passed whenever they went for a drive. His dad's ability to recall those details now were long gone but his infatuation with automobiles was still fully intact. As they would walk, his son would ask: "Do you like that one?" "What about the color of this one?" "Would you ride in a car that small?" The questions were endless; the quality of time spent together was immeasurable.

Each of us has the right to our own opinions, and we need to be respectful of our loved one's even when it differs greatly from ours. In the past we might have had strong differences in our thoughts and ideas; but this time, let them have ownership of their opinions. Show respect for what our loved ones think and be thankful that they still have the ability to express these personal beliefs. Besides, if we weren't able to get them to see our point of view before their illness, I think it's extremely unlikely we would agree now. Most of our loved ones will probably continue to have a mind of their own.

The first time my dad had a serious fall, he broke his neck. He was fitted for a special neck brace to immobilize and protect the cervical fractures. Since he was not supposed to walk any distance without the brace, it was decided that a bedside commode would address the problem of his getting up during the night, without the brace, to go to the toilet. Also, while he was in rehab, the therapists said he needed to start using a walker as he had very poor balance.

My dad was not able to understand the necessity of using a walker. To him, it was a nuisance that he occasionally used only to humor me. And very likely, that was only when I was around. Any time, without exception, that I discovered him toddling around without it, I voiced my concern saying, "I'm just worried that you're going to fall again." He would then make a poor attempt to reassure me with his same smirk and snappy comeback, "I don't plan on falling." For him, this comment was partly to console me as well as a justification for not needing to have a walker in the first place.

The whole concept of "accidents" and importance of safety were simply beyond his mental capacity to comprehend. When the doctor cautioned us about the serious repercussions if he were to fall again before his cervical vertebrae had healed completely, I think he regarded the information akin to a science fiction story. Interesting…but not real.

A few months after my dad returned to his apartment from rehab, his girlfriend came down with a cold or something. Nothing serious but he thought it would be beneficial for her to have a bedside commode. You can only begin to imagine my reaction when I found out that he took his over to her apartment.

"How on earth did you get it down both of those two long halls with your walker?" I asked.

"I just carried it," he said matter-of-factly.

"And you walked all the way there and back without your walker!" I said in total disbelief.

"Well, …yeah," he said to me with a genuinely puzzled look.

I felt both shocked and horrified and yet my dad acted as if I had just asked him the most preposterous questions he had ever heard in his entire life. It's easy for caregivers to make senseless comments when we find ourselves in total disbelief of something a loved one has said or done. In hindsight I realized that for all practical purposes, my remarks were mostly a bunch of nonsense that ended up sounding like an interrogation. Of course, he saw nothing wrong with what he had done. To him, it was all perfectly logical and absolutely the right thing to do. He was thinking only of her.

My dad was always thinking of others with a willingness to help them in any way he could. I finally realized he wasn't rebelling, deliberately breaking any of the "rules," or trying to upset me. He liked to please me and everyone else. He was just that kind of guy!

This was another lesson for me in understanding impaired judgment, thinking, and reasoning. I could plaster his apartment with hot pink signs as reminders to take and use his walker. But fussing, scolding, nagging, or explaining would make little or no difference, other than to leave both of us feeling pretty frustrated. I learned that it didn't do any good for me to be upset so I decided to feel grateful. I began to see these times as perfect opportunities to express gratitude upon finding him safely upright – with or without his walker. And I was especially grateful that the essence of my dad's thoughtful, caring, and considerate nature had remained intact despite his cognitive problems.

Our loved ones did not choose to have dementia, but they do. This is just part of who they are now. It is up to each of us to decide how we will perceive them, demonstrate our love, and value them as unique individuals. As caregivers, we do have a choice.

Margaret was one of the calmest, most accepting caregivers I've ever known. She visited her mother Edith at the nursing home on a daily basis. Although she was both stressed and brokenhearted that her mother had Alzheimer's, Margaret set a wonderful example for any caregiver to follow.

As Edith's dementia progressed, she became extremely outgoing and completely uninhibited. She hugged everybody, everywhere, and said exactly what she thought. In the same way as most people with Alzheimer's, there was no filtering of emotional expressions. It was not unusual for her to burst into a song or dance, regardless of who or what was happening around her. Seldom was the singing or her opinionated comments quiet or discreet. And she didn't just sing or dance — she enthusiastically entertained. At times, without any hesitation or even the slightest hint of rudeness, Edith loudly pointed out with great amusement the lady with the "big butt" as well as what she declared to be "the ugliest baby" she ever saw.

Deep down, I know at times it was somewhat distressing to Margaret, but she never viewed it as a problem needing to be solved. She fully accepted and understood the changes in her mother's personality and the loss of her social graces. Every time with the utmost sincerity, and occasionally with an apologetic tone, Margaret responded to her mother's antics with a warm smile and simple comment, "That's my Mom!"

> **"For after all, the best thing we can do when it is raining is to let it rain."**
> **—Henry Wadsworth Longfellow**

·

Chapter 6

A Caregiver's Magical Mantra

One morning I was at one of the Alzheimer's Memory Cafés, usually a program offered free of charge in local communities, where people with dementia can attend with their care partners for socialization, games, and other activities. Before the meeting started, I was visiting with some of the couples there when a woman rushed up to me and blurted out, "I know you! You're the lady that taught me about DIRM!" She went on to explain that she heard me talk and learned "how to do it" at an Alzheimer's caregiver's educational program she had recently attended and that this was her favorite take-away. This recognition made me both pleased and proud. That was also the day I discovered that in many of the circles of caregivers, the word and lessons of this newly created mantra was spreading fast. During that year, it was rare for me to speak to any group on a dementia-related topic without taking a few minutes to explain the enchanting principles of a coping technique for dementia family caregivers called DIRM, an acronym for "Does It Really Matter?"

In the past I would often read or hear a specialist on aging suggest that caregivers can manage a potential outburst by just taking a deep breath, thinking about the situation for a minute, and calmly asking themselves "Does It Really Matter?" In my experience I have found that when caregivers have the composure to follow through all those steps and are calm enough to verbalize the question, then they are probably already in a somewhat peaceful place. And they have likely figured out the answer to that question on their own. But for the rest of us who have trouble finding tranquility amidst the daily emotionally packed hurdles, we need something with more muscle. Hence, many of us came to embrace the magical power of DIRM. This acronym signifies much more than a word or a question. DIRM is the perfect mantra for dementia caregivers. It serves as both a philosophy as well as a mental exercise that can greatly minimize or even prevent many of the upsets and daily frustrations that caregivers encounter.

I can't honestly recall what was happening at that exact moment that I discovered the full value of using DIRM. What I do remember is how it lightened my mood and helped me to keep things in perspective. From that day on, it became my trustworthy mantra. At that time in my life, my dad and I were both going through a lot of changes and adjustments. Although remaining calm, patient, and loving was at the top of my daily to-do list, seldom did I successfully maintain all these charming qualities by day's end. Practically every day something happened to test my patience, those "storms in a teacup," small events which caregivers perceive as a much bigger concern and are so good at blowing the situation totally out of proportion.

At one time, I thought it might have started the evening I came home from work and found the 8' ladder set up in the living room right in front of the fireplace. After my dad moved in, he was frequently getting up on chairs and changing out light bulbs, usually not because they were burnt out but to replace them with ones with a higher wattage. We had already had one near fire in his bedroom, but there were lots of other problems with this, too. My first concern manifests when I see an eighty-year-old person standing on a stool or a chair; I immediately think of fractured hips! My other issue was that he would often turn the bulbs the wrong direction, then since he thought they were just kind of stuck he would use brute strength causing them to break off in the fixture, leaving glass all over my wood floors for him or my dogs to unsafely walk through.

So, I had finally made a rule – No standing on chairs or stools. And that evening he had clearly broken the rule by using a ladder. I got so upset when I saw it, and all I could think about was easily how he could have fallen and not only broken his hip, but also cracked his head on the fireplace hearth. When I confronted him, he became very indignant, almost belligerent, telling me that I never said he couldn't use a ladder to climb up on. In his mind he had in fact followed the rules. He had not stood on a chair or a stool.

I tried hard to calm myself down realizing that he was unharmed. He had followed the rules, at least in his mind. On the other hand, I had not been specific and exact. This had not been an intentional act of defiance but a result of the dementia which caused his impaired judgment. He was not able to make logical connections or understand implied directions and statements. Again, and again, I kept silently asking myself, does it really matter?

As I later recalled the incident, I recognized that while a few seeds of this coping technique might have been planted, there were no fruitful blooms. Otherwise, it would not have taken me almost the entire evening before I completely regained my composure. I had tried to maintain a different outlook in hopes of maintaining a sense of serenity but pondering the question repeatedly as a question was not effective, at least not for me.

I've come to presume that this whole DIRM thing actually emerged accidently one Saturday morning when I was cooking breakfast for my dad. For some crazy reason, I remember standing with a big knife chopping up veggies for an omelet. It was one of his favorite breakfasts. He sauntered into the kitchen with an amused look and sly grin. Then he proceeded to tell me with great excitement that he had decided to buy his new girlfriend an engagement ring for Christmas.

This "girlfriend" was a lady whom he met and played cards with at the senior center. Occasionally, they went out to dinner, a movie, or a social gathering at her church. But marriage? I did not see this coming! I clearly remember putting the knife down, taking a deep breath, and trying to make sense of all of this in my mind. I told Dad that he needed to help me understand how this would work. Neither of them was able to drive a car; and if they wanted to go "out," I was their designated driver. He lived with me so that I could take care of him. She had medical problems which had prompted her to live with her daughter. "So, where would you live since you both need someone to help you?" I asked.

Evidently, he had already given that some thought because he immediately responded, "She really likes our house. I thought she could just move in with me, and you could take care of both of us." There was no punch line. He was serious!

And I "could take care of both" of them. I'm pretty positive those words were the catalyst that nudged me to the edge of an emotional explosion. Suddenly, I felt like my head was spinning and I was about to lose my last ounce of patience. Too many personal events had already occurred in too short a period. Somedays it was hard enough just to take care of myself

As I leaned against the kitchen counter, I begin quietly repeating — actually it was more like mumbling — those four words ever so slowly. Does- it- really- matter? Does- it- really- matter? Of course, intellectually I knew the honest answer, but my heart was still trying to convince the front half of my brain that controls my emotions and impulsive behaviors.

Then I went from kind of humming each of those words, to slowly chanting, **DIRM…DIRM…DIRM**. At some point, I had ended up standing in somewhat of a meditative pose with the palms of my hands facing up. Before I knew it, I was smiling and amazingly calm. I believe this was the birth of this laughable, meditation.

To this day, I'm still not sure if it's the chanting or that this technique makes us stop and step back from a situation long enough to put things into a proper perspective. Quite honestly, I think it's a smidgeon of both. For one thing, it is almost impossible to recite this effective mantra without having a smirk or smile sneak onto your face. When we take the time to start with DIRM to slow us down and remind us to think for a moment about that one essential question, "Does it really matter?" <u>before</u> reacting or responding, we would find that all too often the answer is a resounding "No." It doesn't matter at all.

Think about how many times caregivers get upset about really stupid stuff. It bothers us when our loved one is wearing a coat when it's 100°, asking us the same question 20 times, or helping in ways that are <u>not</u> helpful. This is just a short list of common annoyances that tend to happen repeatedly, none of which we have the power to change. However, we can change how *we* respond. There are going to be "battles," but when we let our minds briefly pause and follow the principles of DIRM, we tend to choose our words and actions more wisely.

I have shared the details of this calming and coping technique with countless family members at support group meetings, educational programs, and community presentations. Almost as soon as a caregiver learns about the principles of DIRM, they totally embrace the term. It becomes part of their daily vocabulary. I've even seen families make cards to carry, refrigerator signs, carved wooden plaques, and key tags, all bearing the letters, DIRM.

The subject of DIRM comes up frequently during discussions at caregivers' support group meetings. It might be that it's an especially popular term there because these families completely relate to the stress and emotions. Once when we were getting ready to start a meeting, a woman rushed in looking completely exasperated. Without missing a beat, she quickly explained that the entire past week had been "one DIRM thing after another." You can probably imagine the laughter that ensued.

Another time a caregiver was reiterating the same concern which he had shared for the past few months. It greatly disturbed him that his wife insisted on sleeping in her clothes, and he could still not get her to put on her pajamas. As if on cue, several other caregivers started playfully chanting "**DIRM... DIRM...DIRM**," continuing until the room was once again filled with laughter. I think at last, he realized that this was a problem only for him. There are no pajama police that go around checking to ensure people are properly dressed for bed. It didn't hinder her sleep, she was willing to put on clean clothes the next day, and, by all indications, seemed quite comfortable spending the night in her day clothes.

Although it's difficult at times, we need to accept that our loved ones are not going to change. Things are never going to be the way they used to be. Choosing to see situations with a different perspective improves everyone's attitudes and temperaments. Also, you are more likely to achieve a favorable outcome for both of you. Changing your mindset will affect a positive change in theirs.

Certainly, there are going to be times that something really does matter or at least it seems to be important at that exact moment. When you're not sure if a situation or disease related behavior is truly a problem rather than an annoyance, you can still use this technique to clear your mind and refocus.

Stop, step back, let out a deep breath, and then take in a fresh, deep breath of air. Slowly chant D-I-R-M...D-I-R-M...D-I-R-M, in a calming tone of voice. Having your arms rest at your side with the palms of your hands facing up adds an extra Zen dimension to this slightly meditative method.

Afterwards, with a clearer mental attitude, ask yourself any or all of the following questions. This will help you to better determine if your loved one's actions or words do present a genuine concern or issue. Then, you can best decide how or if to proceed, or what steps you need to take next.

- Is this something that is going to matter to you a day from now, a month from now, a year from now?

- For whom is it creating a problem?
- Does my loved one have an unmet need?
- Is this always a problem?
- Who or what might have triggered this behavior?
- Could this behavior be harmful to you, your loved one or to another?

I'm still amazed at the effectiveness of this one, small, simple act. What a wonderful feeling and sense of personal satisfaction when we can control our emotions, maintain our sanity, and keep a sense of humor. These are important things that truthfully do matter and constructively influence our overall well-being.

> **"While we may not be able to control all that happens to us, we can control what happens inside of us."**
> **— Ben Franklin**

Chapter 7

Listening with Our Hearts

Elaine, a loving devoted wife, and an Alzheimer's caregiver shared the following story with me with her eyes rolling and a wait-until-you-hear-what-I-did-now tone of voice. Her husband Jim came to Friends Place several times a week, and she regularly attended the caregiver's support group meetings. This tale was both amusing as well as insightful.

When I asked Elaine if I could use this in the book, she said she would email me, adding, "I hope that my experience will help fellow-caregivers to tune into their loved ones' statements." Here is her story, in her own words, just as she sent it to me.

"The other day as I was getting us ready to go to Friends Place, I gave Jim his shoes. Out of the corner of my eye, I could see that he was having a bit of a struggle getting them on. I said what I usually say, "Jim, if you put your foot on the footrest, you wouldn't have to bend down so far and putting on your shoes would be easier." Jim, of course, ignored my "suggestion."

I went about my business. When it was time to leave, I gave him his jacket and he said that I had given him "thick" socks to wear. I told him that he had on his regular socks and they were not any thicker than any other he wears. He kept insisting that his socks were thick. I found this quite funny and thought this is another one of his strange statements. I kept chuckling about this and when I dropped Jim off at the center, I shared with [the office manager] this very funny (to me) tidbit.

Five hours later when I picked Jim up, we were in the car sharing about our day. When I asked him about his day, he said it was good, but the thick socks were really bothering him and that his feet hurt. I was surprised that he mentioned this since he is so forgetful. I began to think possibly there was a real problem. I told him that when we got home, I would check out his feet. Lo and behold, I discovered that his daylong discomfort did not come from thick socks but from MY shoes (very similar to his). I had mistakenly given him my shoes, which are about 2" shorter and at least 1" narrower. To say I felt just terrible is a gross understatement. My poor dear man suffered in silence all day because his wife did not LISTEN to him.

On thinking this whole situation over, I knew I had learned a valuable lesson in being a caregiver. I did not really watch and listen to my husband. When he said "thick" socks, I should have looked beyond what he said and investigated a little further. I could have spared him much discomfort. I think if Jim had said his feet hurt, I would have checked it out. Also, Jim is not a complainer. The fact that he mentioned the socks several times should have alerted me that something was amiss.

As a caregiver, I do have to look beyond his words and think about who he is. He still communicates pretty well but certainly not like he did before AD. For me, it is so easy to get caught up in what I am doing or what needs to be done next, that I don't pay attention to the present and focus on right now. Hopefully, I will be better at this in the future. I know I won't give him the wrong shoes again!

Moral of my story: *Don't be so quick to discount and dismiss what Jim has to say. To ignore him is dishonoring and it is wrong."*

While caregivers all have good intentions, we sometimes find ourselves listening only half-heartedly. Too often we're doing a hundred other things, or our minds are elsewhere when we should be actively listening. We hear what they are saying but are not consciously listening with the purpose of understanding.

We need to be authentically interested, and actively listen to anything and everything that our loved ones are trying to communicate to us. This is more than listening to their words with our ears. It's about "listening" with our hearts and our eyes so we can "hear" what they are struggling to say to us. As the disease progresses, language skills diminish and so do their words. It's important for us to begin to focus ***now*** on all the ways people communicate – words, body language, sounds, gestures, and emotions.

Taking those few extra minutes to give them our full-undivided attention, and responding with a genuine interest, confirm that they are still valued. It conveys that what they believe and think really does matter. And that they matter to us, too.

Less than a week after Elaine shared her incident, another couple had a similar experience. When they were on their way to the center one morning, Debbie's husband complained that he could hardly breathe because she had shrunk his shorts. Knowing that Harvey had a flair for drama, she dismissed his complaints reassuring him that he was going to be just fine. She told him that his shorts were denim and would loosen up once he had them on for a while. Later that afternoon when Debbie came to pick up Harvey, the staff informed her that he hadn't eaten much at lunch and had complained most of the day about his stomach hurting.

Arriving home, she noticed his shorts were still right on top of the laundry basket in the bedroom. That's when she realized that hers were missing. He had been wearing her blue denim shorts the entire day. She was astonished that he could even get them zipped but now understood why he had been so miserable. Debbie was both appalled and disappointed at how casually she had dismissed his concerns.

There are endless stories just like these from other family caregivers, all filled with sadness because they had not actively listened. And there have been countless regrets from caregivers because complaints from their loved ones had been disregarded rather than investigated. If there are any indications by actions or words that something is amiss, we must take this seriously. Caregivers need to be reminded that although loved ones can dress themselves and appear to be able to do self-care, does not mean that they are consistently doing it properly.

It is not unusual for people with dementia to voice discomfort because they are wearing garments backwards, especially men's briefs or a woman's bra. Shoes are terribly uncomfortable to wear all day when they no longer fit properly, the pair is mismatched with slightly different heel heights, or when they are still stuffed with the paper inside from the time of purchase. And hundreds of stomach aches have occurred from a loved one wearing ill-fitting, outgrown clothes he or she has found in the back of a closet and selected to wear.

Hearing aids can be wedged into the wrong ears, usually with great effort but seldom without causing a huge amount of tenderness. Poor fitting dentures can create sores in the mouth and gums, which in turn will often cause loved ones to lose interest in eating.

Sometimes it is their actions that speak of pain or irritation, rather than their words. When a daughter noticed her mother limping shortly after she became her primary caregiver, her mom said it was just her "old knees" that gave her trouble from time to time. As the months passed, her mother's knees seem to be causing more pain and greater difficulty for her to ambulate. It wasn't until one day when the daughter was finally able to assist her mother with bathing that she discovered the horrifying cause of the problem. It wasn't her knees at all. During the time, her mother had been living alone, she had neglected to trim her toenails. Apparently, they had not been cut for quite a long time and had begun to turn inward, growing into the ball of her foot. It was a wonder her mother could even stand let alone walk. Since her mother had previously taken care of all of her own personal needs and grooming, it never occurred to the daughter to check her feet or nails. In all honesty, rarely does it cross the mind of a caregiver to ask or even check a loved one's nails when the person is seemingly able and independent.

These are all examples of senseless mistakes that occur when we don't listen. And yet it is easy to do. Caregivers are juggling the responsibilities of running households, holding down jobs as well as managing all the personal affairs for at least two people, sometimes more. There are meals to plan, shopping, errands to run, doctor's appointments, cooking, cleaning, and endless lists of chores. However, not paying attention can unnecessarily consume even more time and create new challenges.

There is a distinct difference between hearing words and sounds versus listening and understanding a message. Those times when we hear words but don't really listen will often prevent us from asking the right questions or having the necessary information to communicate effectively in a caring manner. We tend to speak before we think, and we react rather than respond appropriately.

Early one Saturday morning, my Dad and I were at a community arts festival at a local park. Originally, I had planned to go alone. I didn't really have the time to go but was looking for a specific item for my home office. Dad insisted on going along and promised he would keep up with me. I knew he loved going places, so I agreed. Little did I know at the time, that this was only my first mistake.

We had been there about fifteen minutes when Dad asked if I knew where the bathrooms were located. Even if I had been more familiar with the park, there were over 200 booths laid out in and around the trees, in a giant maze. I didn't stop to ask any questions but just turned on my heels and hurried off toward the large building where I was certain the restrooms were located. That was my second mistake. Many of the rows of vendors were dead ends, which just impeded our search. We finally arrived at the building to find that there weren't any restrooms there. That's when I found someone to ask and discovered that they were in the opposite direction from where we had been walking.

Finally, after rushing around for about 10 minutes or so (it really seemed like an hour), we ended up in a parking area where about 20 portable toilets were located. This was not what I had expected.

Turning to my dad I asked, "Can you use one of these?"

"For what?" he said.

"I thought you had to go to the bathroom?"

"I don't have to go. I thought you needed to go after all that coffee you drank this morning."

I wasn't sure whether to laugh, cry, or scream. It was definitely a DIRM (does-it-really-matter) moment. And it was all my fault. I never took the time to ask him any questions. I just reacted. I would have never done the same thing with my sons when they were young or any of my grandchildren. Any normal mother interrogates them first. Can you wait? How bad do you have to go? Didn't you go before we left?

For a long time after the incident with Jim, Elaine would remind all the other caregivers, including me, that "our failings are not a total failing if we learn from them and improve our actions." That morning, I learned many lessons from my failing to actively listen. Hurrying will always take longer. Don't make assumptions. Fathers like to be helpful.

> **"We are so busy doing the urgent that we don't have time to do the important."**
> **— Confucius**

Chapter 8

Are You Real Busy?

The first time I met Beth was in her home. She corrected me at the beginning of our visit to explain this was actually her "son's home," then added, she was grateful to be there and had recently moved from out of state to be nearer her family. She was polite, quiet, and friendly. All of her life, Beth had worked exceptionally hard. In addition to cooking, cleaning, and rearing a huge family, she also worked outside of the home. Now widowed, her home sold, and thousands of miles from her church and friends, she was adjusting to her new life. She was also having to get used to the idea of someone's taking care of her. When Beth told me that she and her daughter-in-law Connie got along fine, I got the distinct impression it was because she was good at being a subservient mother-in-law who understood her place in that household. She lived there but it definitely was not *her* home.

Beth also told me, very privately, that it was hard for her to just sit around and have others do everything for her. Words like "useless," "helpless," and "in the way" came up often in many of our conversations. I knew her daughter-in-law genuinely cared about her and had been the one to originally suggest Beth move-in with them. Unfortunately, Connie made some of the same mistakes as many of us have when caring for a loved one. Sometimes we take our roles as caregivers too seriously, providing care in excess, only to end up unintentionally "overparenting" our parent or even a spouse. While it's nice occasionally to be treated as company or a special guest, it pales in comparison to feeling independent, maintaining a sense of self-worth and being a contributing adult.

Numerous times I tried to talk to Connie about ways in which Beth could help out a little more around the house. Connie enjoyed doing things "for" Beth and said she didn't need any help. For every one of my suggestions, she countered with a litany of reasons as to why it was not feasible. First off, allowing Beth to assist in anyway with cooking was totally out of the question. She had tons of reasons and concerns as to why that was not going to happen. When I hinted at the possibility of Beth's making the salad for dinner or prepping the vegetables, she expressed concerns about her using a sharp knife. The words had hardly come out of my mouth, when she told me that tearing the lettuce leaves by hand was not an option either. Connie also didn't want her dusting for fear she would break something. When I mentioned allowing Beth to help with the laundry by folding clothes, I was informed that she didn't fold anything correctly. Finally, I suggested having her fold only the washcloths and towels. She said that didn't work either. Because Beth didn't fold them the right way, they wouldn't fit in the linen closet. All I could think about and wanted so badly to say was, "Just rearrange the closet!" But I did not say another word, because I knew it wouldn't make any difference. She didn't understand, and it was probably never going to happen, at least not in her home.

When we are caring for loved ones with dementia, it is never about the task. That's where so often, caregivers totally miss the point. Throughout my career, I have upheld that everyone needs to be able to make daily contributions to preserve feelings of self-worth. This becomes even more important when a person is limited, to any extent, either cognitively or physically.

Thank goodness that at least some caregivers understand the importance of participation. They are smart enough to ask, encourage and accommodate their loved ones' offers to help. One evening I was visiting with one of my friends about this topic and lamenting the fact that some caregivers find hundreds of excuses but won't take the time to figure out just one solution to this common dilemma. That's when I learned that a savvy caregiver can never have too many onions. As she told me this loving tale with its own perfect moral, I knew it was too good not to include it in the book and asked if she would please share it —in her own words— for the benefit of other caregivers.

So, my friend Pam asked me to write down this story. It is a story I have told. It is a story born of love and decency and ineptitude with a "eureka" moment. Today, my task is to share one of the little victories we achieved as we walked through this horrendous disease.

Early on there were times when I was surprised and confused by Mom's behavior and thought process. As time moved on and it became obvious that there was something terribly wrong, I found myself in a time of immobilizing sadness and feeling woefully incapable and unskilled in handling what life had dealt. I went from continuing to work while worrying about what was happening at home to taking time off from work and finally, thankfully finding adult day services. During the later stage of that I was able to return to work while Mom went to an adult day center. It became our daily routine - I would take Mom to her "job", I would go to mine, then pick her up in the evening. Once home it was dinner, a little entertainment, bed...all to be repeated the next day.

Mom was never someone who liked to be stagnant. She always wanted to do something. So, my preparing dinner for her was not an option. It became an activity that we would do together. However, as I have a tiny, galley kitchen it was not easy for the two of us to be there at the same time and it frustrated us both (me more so, I'm sure). So, one day I decided to do things differently. I got an onion, a cutting board, her favorite knife and placed all at the end of the counter. During dinner prep it became her contribution to cut and dice the onions. Now, I didn't always need an onion. I didn't always want an onion. But it was important to her that she be productive and make a contribution.

And it was important to me to find a way to eliminate frustration and keep the act of making dinner from taking all evening. Somewhere in this simple process it accomplished that and more as we managed to have conversations that we might not have had otherwise.

As I remember it now, that is one of the more special memories I have of her during that time. If you're reading this, you probably already know that there isn't a lot of good to be remembered about time with this disease.

And you should know, that for a long time, if you came to visit me, you would find containers of onions in my freezer. As I said, I didn't always want or need onions. But she did. And that's all that mattered.

People with dementia usually fall into one of two categories. They either think they can still do everything or have come to believe they can't do anything. And there can be huge downsides to both ways of thinking. Neither way is without consequences if caregivers don't respond appropriately to these feelings and needs. In order for there to be any positive outcomes there must caregiver awareness. Our actions are what enable our loved ones to enjoy any degree of a quality of life.

While our loved ones might think they can do anything and everything, we know differently. When there's a task that they want to do that maybe they did before or think they still can, first try to determine specifically why this is a problem now. Is it a problem for them or for us? Are there safety concerns? Then as we honestly assess their strengths and limitations; we can hopefully build on their remaining abilities. It might mean breaking a task into smaller steps or doing only one part of the task. Perhaps then, the chore can be completed by our loved one successfully and independently, or as independently as possible.

All too often I have seen people with dementia swing much too rapidly from trying to do everything to doing nothing at all. Caregivers should think twice before they roll their eyes or criticize the efforts of a loved one. One reason that people with dementia stop doing is because many things are now too difficult or complicated; they don't understand what they are being asked to do, and mostly they feel as if nothing they do is satisfactory. It is not the actual disease that has made our loved ones feel like they can't do anything. Dementia creates limitations, but the desire to give up while they still have capabilities stems from us. It is often our attitudes and responses which have made them feel unworthy. Their sad and negative feelings are the result of caregivers not sanctioning or presenting opportunities for our loved ones to contribute. When we don't ask or allow them to help, we send a message loud and clear that they are not good enough. It is why they no longer ask or offer to help.

True success in overcoming our loved ones' undeserving attitude of uselessness can be achieved by caregivers sincerely asking one short, simple question; "Are you real busy?" This is always my first and best suggestion when caregivers tell me they can't get their loved-one to do "anything." When we use this approach before asking for help, it tends to work well for several reasons. First it is obviously a question not a demand. It implies they are the ones in control and lets them decide if they are "available" for us. This question demonstrates our confidence in their ability and our belief they are capable or else we wouldn't have asked. It's also successful because it denotes a purpose. Although caregivers might sometimes get a "Why?" response, it's almost certain to be followed up with a "What do you need?" or "How can I help?"

One of the many times I have used it successfully was with a gentleman that was sitting by himself, slumped so far down in the dining room chair that he looked like he could easily slither to the floor despite his large size. The look of despair on his face would fill anyone's heart with sadness. Had I not known better, it would have been easy to assume that he had just loss every last friend and family member. According to the other staff at this memory care community, he had been like this most of the week with no interest in participating in any of the activities or talking with anyone.

As though I had not noticed his despondency, I walked over to him nonchalantly, then asked with just the slightest hint of a plea in my voice, "Are you real busy?" He sat up a bit, looking around as if to confirm that I was in fact speaking to him, then asked what I needed. When I said, I was looking for someone to sharpen some pencils for me, his entire demeanor changed as he set up straight, smiling, and ready to go to work.

From then on, he was my go-to guy for all sorts of tasks for which I needed help. Within the next few months, we very likely had enough sharpened pencils to supply an entire elementary school. A box of new pencils, one pencil sharpener, and a renewed interest in life ...now filled with some purpose.

I mentioned before that I look at things with a "what if it were me?" perspective. Probably few, if any of us, would be willing (certainly not thrilled) to have someone plop down a jar of buttons or bag of beans in front of us and say, "Here, sort these out." All the while this other person is thinking, this is nice and will give them something to do.

Now imagine, having a family member respectfully ask first if you have time --willingness-- to do a task, suggesting that they need *your* help. But it's not merely to sort a bag of mixed beans or a stupid jar of buttons. They are asking if you would please help to pick out just the black beans. Maybe explaining why ...someone in the family doesn't like black beans so you're cooking only the black ones for tonight. Or they are asking if you would find all of the red, white, and blue buttons in this jar so the two of you could craft and decorate a bottle for a patriotic event.

One time I decided to purchase one hundred boxes of instant pudding as giveaways at a marketing event. Each box had a specially designed label adhered to the front with a reminder to caregivers how easy this would be for their loved one to make. They were handed-out at health fairs, a support group meeting; and, I personally gave one box to Beth's daughter in-law.

Caregivers also received some additional instructions for creating some other fabulous nightly desserts which their loved-one could safely and easily make with instant pudding. There are over a dozen flavors available and a multitude of variations. Fresh bananas or canned fruit can be added; whole vanilla wafers or chocolate sandwich cookies crushed-up in a zip lock bag to use in the pudding; and finished with whipped topping, chopped nuts, chocolate chips, and a cherry on top…the variations are endless.

It was a perfect solution to the how-can-I-help-with-dinner question. Think about it. **Anybody** can make instant pudding! No cooking is required. Pre-measured milk just needs to be poured into the bowl. You can't over stir or whip it too much. It's easy and inexpensive. Pour, whisk, and serve and …voila! You have a yummy dessert or snack. All that's left for you to do is thank your loved one for making this special treat and enjoy this simple pleasure together! This is just one example of rethinking possibilities that enable them to contribute and experience feelings of independence.

We do many tasks each day with little or no thought. But the actual steps and overall process can be overwhelming for people with short-term memory problems and is only easy if they are able to remember where items are located and to understand the names and meaning of all the words. Here are a few more tips caregivers might consider for supporting a loved one's desire to help with some of the everyday household chores:

- Setting the table can be simplified by laying out the items on the counter in groups of the order in which they would be placed. Using placemats on the table defines the setting location. Using cloth napkins at meals not only saves some trees but provides extra items to be folded.
- Additional washcloths and kitchen towels can be purchased inexpensively from a dollar store for folding and kept in a basket on standby.

- When they want to sweep the front porch or backyard patio, hand them the broom to prevent frustration or distraction from their trying to find it.
- Set aside time once a week to "help" a loved one make a favorite dish or dessert. One daughter shared that it's much like a cooking show on television but a lot messier. She pre-measured and did most of the prep-work but allowed her mother to superficially get all the credit. It brought back fond memories of her childhood when her mother was teaching her to cook. There might have been flour and spills everywhere, but the kitchen was filled with laughter, wonderful aromas, and moments to cherish.
- Out in the yard, prop up the rake against a ready-to-fill leaf bag or box. One son shared that it gave his father hours of satisfaction. So much so, that when the son let the cat out for the night, he re-scattered all the leaves to ensure his dad would have additional days of pleasure and purpose.
- An old-fashioned feather duster can be handy for "cleaning" furniture, lamps, drapes as needed for tidiness or a daily sense of purpose.

Let them lend a helping hand. This is not a suggestion. It is a must-do. At least it is a mandatory directive for any caregiver committed to preserving a loved one's dignity. As I write this, I can hear many of you in my head both agreeing and disagreeing. Caregivers seem to recognize the importance of letting them assist but in the same breath bemoan the fact that when they help, it's usually not helpful. It takes more time, they don't' do it right, or two minutes later they're off doing something else.

I do understand because I had those same thoughts and feelings while I was adapting to the role of being a full-time caregiver. Fortunately, I was able to change my perspective so my words as well as my actions were in alignment with my true beliefs. Life must be filled with meaning and purpose.

One Saturday morning before I knew what was happening, my dad decided to help me by filling the bird feeders. He was taking the large bird seed containers out of the garage while at the same time telling me what he planned to do. It really wasn't a suggestion or even an offer to assist me, but rather a pronouncement. It was a demonstration of his desire to contribute and do something meaningful. This was an activity with purpose.

There were a number of feeders, each different in size and design, throughout the yard. So, it did take time. Dad liked doing things around the house which he thought would be helpful to me. But every single time, it took twice as long to get him set up than it would for me to do it myself. And every single time, there was a huge mess with bird seed spilling all over the patio and the grass. As you might guess, I wasn't always the patient, loving daughter I wanted to be. It was just one more frustration added to my already stressful life. Inevitably it took up more time, out of an already too short weekend, than I felt I had to spare.

This is the part of the story where I wish I could tell you that I was suddenly able to draw on my decades of experience and knowledge and adjust my attitude. Well, that didn't happen. At least not exactly that way. It was my grandson who unknowingly changed my perspective of the entire situation and allowed me to see everything differently.

What did happen a month or so later was my grandson was spending Saturday with me at my house while Dad was away with friends. We were outside and he was helping me in the yard with gardening, watering, and feeding the birds. I spread newspaper on the patio so we could sit on the ground to fill the feeders together. Like most four-year-old kids he was very independent. After some gentle persuasion on my part and a lot of resistance on his part, he allowed me to "help" him. By the time we finally finished, the entire area on and around the patio was shrouded in bird seeds. I knew that I would be dealing with the stray seeds sprouting up a profusion of weeds throughout my lawn for months. But I didn't mind. He was very proud of his accomplishments, and we had a really good time that afternoon. But later that evening it finally dawned on me. Why was this any different than when Dad sometimes made a mess? Another day of lessons learned. The rewards do outweigh extra efforts. The desire to help is ageless. Feeling useful is invaluable.

Beginning at a young age and throughout our childhoods, we want to be a grown-up. We like the thought of being an adult, making our own decisions, keeping busy, being productive, and helping others. We do not want to sit on the sidelines and watch life; we want to live life. Those feelings and desires do not change.

I hope when caregivers read this chapter, they will fully realize what is truly at the heart of this message. It is much more than merely allowing them to lend a helping hand when they ask or offer. It is about us creating opportunities for our loved ones to do meaningful activities which bring them pleasure, create a sense of purpose, and provide a feeling of accomplishment. It is easier than we think! Remember that some caregivers have already discovered joy and contentment can be realized from a freezer filled with chopped onions, unwanted weeds in a beautiful yard, or a small box of instant pudding. How busy is your loved one? What might you do differently today to help them?

> **"Joy, feeling one's own value,
> being appreciated and loved by others,
> feeling useful and capable of production are all factors of
> enormous value for the human soul."**
> **—Maria Montessori**

Reprinted with permission by Michael Olaf Montessori Company with approval of family.

Chapter 9

Create an Illusion of Control

Mornings were seldom a good time for either Janet or her husband Jake. Due to Jake's diagnosis of Lewy Body Dementia, his world had become a mix of hallucinations and distorted reality. It was mentally exhausting and gradually he lost all interest in life. Jake had started getting up much later in the mornings, taking long afternoon naps, and retiring each night right after dinner. It was not unusual for him to sleep sixteen to twenty hours a day. Naturally, the more he slept, the more tired he became; and his energy level decreased to a point of serious concern. He was missing meals, losing weight, and taking his medications sporadically.

For a while it wasn't really an issue, just a tragic aspect of the disease. Although Janet was still employed full time, she was able to work at home. In the beginning, the sleeping-in and naps gave her the time she needed to do her job. Soon she realized that this was surely not normal, even for someone with dementia. Jake's excessive sleeping, loss of initiative, and lack of cognitive stimulation was preventing him from having any quality of life.

While Janet was doubtful that he would have the stamina or the willingness to attend an adult day program, she took the chance and enrolled him. Jake surprised everyone. From the very first day, he thoroughly enjoyed being at the center and talking with the other guys about history, sports, and travel. But for Janet, getting him up and out of bed every morning was a huge and frustrating challenge. Neither of them ever arrived there in a good mood.

Then one morning they both came through the door all hugs, sweetness, and smiles. Something had obviously changed and changed for the good. When I asked her about it, she said she had taken my advice. "My advice?" I questioned. Janet explained that after attending a presentation I gave at a support group meeting she had decided to follow my suggestion. I had urged each of those attending to find creative solutions for some of the challenges that each one faced on a daily basis.

Janet explained that in order to get Jake to the center in time for her to return home for her workday, he had to get up every morning at 9:30. On this particular morning, she went in at 9:00 am and gently roused him. When he grumbled, she asked him if he would like to sleep for another 30 minutes. He was shocked but pleasantly surprised. "Well, yeah, can I really?" he asked. "Sure," she said, "we might have to hurry a little, but I just thought this morning you might like to stay in bed a little while longer."

Jake was willingly awake and up out of bed at 9:30, his normal time. He appreciated that his wife had allowed him to sleep in that morning. It was as if he himself had been able to decide when to get up. He was in a good mood and ready to start his day. The positive outcome was one blissful couple.

This is one of my favorite real-life love stories. It is such a wonderful example of a caregiver choosing dignity and creativity over an imposed showing of domination. She spawned the perception of Jake being in control and it was a win-win result for both of them. Doesn't everybody love stories with happy endings!

We all want to be in control. You do. I do. And so, do those with dementia. Being in control is an essential psychological need that each of us has as a child or an adult. Undeniably some people have a much stronger need to be frequently in total control whereas it might be less important to other people with different personalities. Just as with any of our basic needs —like food, water, or our need for affection— each of us require different amounts in order to feel fulfilled.

For most of us, "feeling" in control is more important than actually "being" in control. With dementia it is often much more about trust than it is power. And it is always a give-and-take process. As caregivers, we soon learn that we can achieve greater successes when there is a balance of power and trust or at least a perceived sense of balance.

For persons with any type of dementia, the need to feel in control is central to their well-being. There are already too many changes taking place in their lives. Their world keeps getting smaller and more complicated because of their loss of memory and the impact of other symptoms. All of which makes them feel powerless.

In order to feel in control, people need a sense of certainty and understanding. It helps when life, people (including caregivers like us), and events are predictable and consistent, none of which commonly occurs when someone has dementia.

Seldom can they totally discern what is expected of them or what they can anticipate. They do not have the benefit of remembering plans, rules, rituals, or other words of comfort that are necessary to develop this sense of certainty, or the ability to fully trust others, with so much happening in their lives.

Before, our loved ones were used to being in charge and in control of almost everything in their lives. Now they can easily feel as if they have no control over anything. Even when they trust others, they will likely still worry. It is up to us to continue to remind and reassure, to give them a sense of confidence and peace of mind.

My dad used to say that seniors are all a bunch of worrywarts. I do agree that most people with memory problems definitely worry way too much. As caregivers, it helps if we can understand why they ask us hundreds of times about something that needs to be done even if it is days or weeks away. That stuff seems to stay stuck in their minds.

Although they often forget that we do always manage to take care of whatever the issue or mission is, they stay firmly focused on it and continue to remind us. Sometimes even adding, "There's no hurry; I just thought I'd better check." Then they check again, again and again. I think it's one of those many mysteries concerning the seemingly selective things they are able to recall. Of course, even when we understand why they do it, it can still make us a tad crazy.

Most of us underestimate the importance of giving them choices. We take for granted the hundreds of decisions we make every single day. Ultimately, we choose if and when we are going to get up, go to bed at night, and we are confronted with countless other decisions in between. Some are certainly more important than others, but nevertheless they are ***our*** decisions. There are probably days that most of us get so tired of having to make yet another decision that we just want somebody else to decide. But I would doubt that any of us would want another person to make every one of our decisions all the time... forever? Probably not.

As the disease progresses, the normal opportunities for them to have choices become increasingly limited, and we will just naturally be making more of their daily decisions. Still, in order to maintain their dignity, we must allow them to be involved or at least feel as if they have a voice in some of the everyday life decisions. Even making small, insignificant decisions throughout the day, keeps life in balance and enables them to have a sense of control. Expressing their preferences and desires creates feelings of self-worth and helps them to continue feeling like a respected adult.

Choices do need to be limited as not to overwhelm. Open-ended questions can cause much anxiety, frustration for both of you and will seldom deliver truthful answers. It will most likely result in a common retort such as, "I don't know," or "whatever you think." Giving them only two choices is a good number that enables them to comfortably make a decision. We should present only those options which lead to ***our*** desired outcome. I would never ask someone with dementia if they want to bathe, because I already know that 99% of the time the answer will be "NO!" By asking if they want to take a shower now or wait about an hour, allows the person to feel some sense of control.

One caregiver figured out an approach that worked well with her husband. Carol would calmly say, "We need to get cleaned up." Then, she would ask her husband Frank if he wanted to take his shower first before she took her shower. It made it sound like a routine activity for each of them, not a task that was only about him. It wasn't a command or any indication that he needed bathing. Just a matter-of-fact comment that got the job done without an incident. It enabled him actively to take part in the decision-making process by allowing him to have some input.

At times we might think it's easier or faster to just make decisions for them. And it usually is both easier and faster. But that's not the point. Even those times when we don't offer them a choice because we already know what their decision will be, generates a lost opportunity for them to exercise their sense of control. Sometimes, we need to step back and ask ourselves if this is worth risking a loss of dignity. How much more time does it really take to ask, "Do you want sweet tea for lunch?" rather than just setting it on the table in front of them like we probably do every day? This might sound like such a little thing and it is. But little things do add up to be big things. In the end, isn't it usually those small things that matter most?

As it should be, we are the ones that ultimately have hold of the reins. However, it's going to be beneficial to all when we loosen up on the reins and finally recognize that we must give in order to receive. When we get into the habit of giving up some of the power, we gain more of the control. It becomes productive for us, respectful of them, and successful for both.

> **"Let everything be done as if it makes a difference."**
> —William James

Chapter 10

Permission to Be Good Enough

The instructions were clear and simple. **Step #1- Identify: Check each one of the boxes below that is a source of guilt for you.** So, I did. Whoa…for some strange reason I was astounded to find that I had checked every single box on the first page of the worksheet in addition to a couple more. In total, eight out of the fifteen. Sure, I knew that I felt guilty about some stuff. I'm a caregiver. We all feel guilty. I shouldn't have been surprised. I've been working in this field long enough clearly to understand that Alzheimer's caregivers do "Guilt" better than anyone in the world. At the end of the list on the bolded line, next to the box marked "**Other**," I added my own unique reason for guilt, "Because I Know Better."

As a follow-up to one of my Alzheimer's caregiver support group presentations, I held an Action Workshop for Overcoming Guilt. At the request of a family caregiver, I developed an interactive class, specifically to address the issue of spousal and family caregiver guilt. Rather than merely talking about this topic, several others agreed it would be beneficial for caregivers to be able to take the time to sit down in a group setting. This would allow them to recognize their personal sources of guilt, to set goals, and to create action steps. Together we also discussed possible obstacles and identified potential resources.

After the workshop, I decided that this was a good opportunity for me, too, to realistically assess the source of my own guilty feelings. I'm a firm believer in acceptance, and I do know that especially with dementia, some things are just what they are. Our loved ones, those with dementia, are not capable of changing to suit us. With that understanding, we need a way to step back and honestly discern between the things that can be changed versus and what cannot. Sort of like the Serenity Prayer, but with lots of specific details and all written down to form an individualized, explicit plan of action.

Ever since I became a caregiver for my dad, I have been terribly disillusioned by the number of mistakes I have made. Worse yet, I've made many of them more than once. After all, I thought, here I am with all this great experience, knowledge, an abundance of patience, and a sincere love for working with people with memory impairment. So, I figured I should be pretty good at this. I was naïve enough to think that since I usually excelled at my "day" job, that maybe I could even be the perfect caregiver. And when I wasn't (which was often), I still kept thinking that at least I *should* be the best. Oh my, there's that word -"should"- that sparks guilty feelings faster than the speed of light.

While it can be easy to fall into a pool of guilt, it is usually slippery trying to get out and takes a lot of sincere effort. Each of us can begin by taking our personal feelings into consideration. I'm not just talking about guilt but all the other emotions we feel, too. Why do we feel the way we do at times? Other people don't need to understand, only us. These are our feelings and there might be a lifetime of events that come into play. So, we need to take ownership and not allow others to be telling us how we should or shouldn't feel. Hmm, there's that should word again.

It has always amazed me how people can be incredibly opinionated and knowledgeable about something they know so little about. Friends and family members tend to give a lot of advice and "helpful" suggestions even when they have not a clue as to how difficult it is to be a full-time caregiver. While their job allocates time for breaks, lunch, and vacations to allow them to recharge, many family caregiver's "work" days do not.

Kindly ignore those in your life that are quick to share what you should do, what you ought to have done, what they would have done. Politely listen but don't even be tempted to respond. Accept that others will not always agree with your actions or your decisions. When my boys were very young, most of our friends had not started their families, but from them I received countless words of advice. My mother would often lovingly tell me that she believed the best mothers in the world, were those without children. It's much easier to make decisions that do not affect your life in any way. Others will not understand, nor will they need to deal with any consequences that might arise.

I remember once being told by a family therapist that I was a perfectionist. I just started laughing. "Yea... sure" I said, "You wouldn't say that if you ever saw my house or my desk at work." Then, I realized that neither my husband nor my son was laughing. With a serious, almost I-hate-to-tell-you look, they were both nodding their heads in agreement with the doctor.

That day I learned that being a "perfectionist" is a far cry from being perfect, and the two words should not be confused. It's not a good thing to be a perfectionist as they are inclined to refuse to accept or be content with anything short of perfection. This becomes problematic since expectations for themselves or others are unrealistic, and goals unattainable.

The number one source of guilt, for the vast majority of dementia caregivers, stems from the desire to be perfect, even though many, maybe even most, are satisfied to be less than perfect in all other aspects of their life. I think it's because we are all willing to have lower personal standards for us but find that unacceptable for the ones we love so deeply and for whom we are caring. This is just the tip of the iceberg. As caregivers, we can find a multitude of reasons to feel guilty.

Each day we can only make the best decision that we can, based on what we know at that given moment. Hopefully, tomorrow if we know better, we will be better. Figure out what is your personal best and let that be your measure of standard. Don't compare yourself to other caregivers or another's situations.

Hundreds of times we've heard, if you've seen one person with Alzheimer's, you've seen <u>one</u> person with Alzheimer's. But this same statement is every bit as true when we are talking about caregivers. Each of us has a different personality, skill set, financial situation, knowledge base, temperament, stress threshold, and support system. And, of course, the list goes on but I'm sure you get the idea.

Once when a woman was trying to be strong and minimize the stress and difficulties of her situation, she mentioned that her life was not nearly as bad as what some of the other women in the group were dealing with. I just kept thinking, "Oh, my gosh! That's like saying one broken leg isn't a big deal because it could have been two." Both situations are tragic, each on its own without any comparison.

No matter how much we do, we still have the mindset that we should be able to do more. It might seem like a "36 Hour Day" at times, but it's not. Even if the days were twice as long, it would still not be long enough to do all the things we so often think that need to be done.

We feel guilty about making mistakes, losing our patience, hating the tasks of caregiving, or spending any time away from our loved one. We feel guilty about all sorts of things we didn't do or things we should have done. On rare moments, some of us even find ourselves feeling guilty about <u>not</u> feeling guilty.

Take a minute to evaluate your guilty feelings. List anything and everything that makes you feel guilty. Then, go back through the list and determine how frequently. Does it make you feel guilty all the time, some of the time or just occasionally? Narrow your list down to the heavy hitters and then pick out three that seem to cause you the worst frustration or are a constant source of guilt for you. There's no point in trying to deal with too many at a time. Once you get the first ones under control, it gets a bit easier and you can add more, a few at a time.

There are other questions we need to ask, too. What are our needs? What support systems do we have in place? Are our expectations realistic – for us and for them? What are the strengths and limitations of our loved-one, and what are ours?

Next, you'll need to set goals and figure out specific actions to attain them. Don't treat this like a New Year's resolution and get too carried away. Saying I'm not going to ever lose my temper anymore is like resolving to lose 20 pounds in a month by going to the fitness center and working out every day. It's not going to happen.

Occasionally we deal with conflicting emotions. Just about all of us are doing this purely because we love this person who needs us and choose to be there for them. And yet, at the same time, it is not unusual for a caregiver to wish it were over, not love them in the same way as in the past or decide they don't want to do this anymore. These are normal feelings, but you need to hear it from others that you trust and admire. Reading it once in a book or having one person tell you is not going to be emotionally helpful.

Through years of working with countless families, I've discovered something heartwarming. Even when a son or daughter stepped-up to care for an estranged parent, was "elected" by other siblings that were married/too busy/had children, or was simply not the favorite child (nor was this their favorite parent); at some point during this incredibility difficult journey, a mutual love and respect surfaced.

The tricky thing about guilt is that it doesn't just slam us down all at once. Early on we start feeling only slightly guilty about one or two little things, often something we wish we could have done better or differently. Then we become like teapots on the stove. Each added feeling of anger or resentment starts the water boiling. There might be hurtful and irritated thoughts about shattered dreams for the future; other family members not helping; giving up our jobs, hobbies or interests; not being able to spend time with our grandchildren, our friends or members of our church not staying in touch; or feeling alone and isolated. Then comes the tsunami of emotion that everyone of us has felt, that too often goes unsaid. "I want my life back the way it used to be!" It's more than enough to boil all the water from our pot, spilling it everywhere.

Hopefully, each of us will acknowledge our guilty feelings before there is a serious concern for our physical or emotional well-being or that of our loved one. When guilt is not properly addressed, it can become a much bigger problem, often developing into uncontrollable rage or anger, deep depression, or a type of resentment that results in a total lack of empathy. Guilt also creates additional stress, which leads to a multitude of critical health problems. And, we all know that a caregiver's stress level is already off the charts.

Most people outside of a support group are horrified when we say or do something out of character. Without any hesitation they will dole out a litany of reasons to explain why they believed our behavior was inexcusable. They tell us, as though we don't already know in our hearts, that our loved ones are doing the best that they can. We, too, wish that we would not raise our voice when we're upset, get frustrated or angry. Even when others choose to say nothing, their looks of dismay say it all. No one else can comprehend the stress and daily challenges unless they have lived it.

It took me a while not to get upset with others when they would promptly point out any of my shortcomings. I had to remind myself that they said it with the best intentions. But it was still hurtful and compounded my feelings of guilt every time I felt myself stumble on this journey. Now when that happens, I recognize that family, friends, or other non-caregivers mean well, so my action step is to just smile sincerely and say nothing. All the while, I'm thinking, "You just have no idea."

Some days our actions, words and deeds will simply have to be "good enough" even when we might think it wasn't very good at all.

We are not perfect; therefore, mistakes are permissible. My dad used to tell me that "All we can do is the best we can do." So, if at any given moment, we are doing our best, then we must know in our heart, it is enough. The only requirements for this job are for us to be loving, kind, respectful …and good enough.

> **"To think is easy. To act is hard.**
> **But the hardest thing in the world is to act**
> **in accordance with your thinking."**
> **—Johann Wolfgang von Goethe**

Chapter 11

In Their Own Words

I was standing at the sink just listening, frozen in time, as my eyes filled to the brim with tears. "Are you okay?" my husband asked as he walked into the kitchen. I smiled and tilted my head in the direction of the living room where my dad sat with my cousin Greg, reading aloud from his Life Stories book. I was filled with such great joy and emotion that it was hard to speak. "That's my dad, my real dad," I said. It was all that I could manage to say and all that mattered at that moment.

Mike and I had only been married a few years at that time. He had never known my father before dementia. Nor was he aware of my dad's reputation as a revered storyteller, never missing an opportunity to share with his family the adventures of his youth. The bigger the audience, the grander the retelling. The addition of grandsons' wives, great grandchildren, and extended family members turned many of these story times into humorous mini performances. His laughter and delight spilled over to all who gathered around him, willing to listen, ready to be entertained.

A few days earlier, both of my cousins had arrived for a visit from out of state, and they had not seen my dad, their only uncle, in a long time. They were used to the "Uncle Charley" who talked non-stop, laughed a lot, and shared endless stories. Instead they found a man, with little memory of them or his past, who sat quietly unless spoken to. Dad still remembered a few basic facts about some of his earlier life and childhood, but almost no details. Beyond basic social conversations, there was little exchange of words or information in any dialogues.

But then, on that day for a few hours, all of that changed. That was when I realized firsthand that a Life Story Book has the power somehow, almost magically, to bring a loved one back to us, if even only for a short while. It was especially meaningful in many ways for all of us. Dad wasn't just reading the words; he was reliving those moments in time. Pausing mid-way through a story, he would laughingly add, "Boy, wait until you hear this one," or "Oh, this is a really good story." Memories and people long forgotten suddenly returned as he read these stories from his past, all now recorded on paper using his own words, his own language. Best of all, we got to take this journey with him. Together we listened with a mixture of both happiness and sadness at stories about beloved family members who are no longer with us. The stories momentarily brought them vividly back into his life and ours. Despite age, time, or disease, we deeply connected as one family -- one emotion.

The timing of this discovery could not have been any better. My father had reached the stage in this horrible disease rendering him unable to comprehend any structure of family relationships. Grandsons, great-grandchildren, nieces, nephews, and at times even me, his only child, were all mixed-up together. With no distinction of one being different from another, we all existed in the same cognitive bucket in his mind labeled "Relations."

During the first couple of days of my cousins' visit, little snippets and details of his past had been lovingly doled out in hopes that something would rekindle at least a few of his long-term memories. Sometimes he would pretend to remember and other times he would apologetically smile and say that it was probably too long ago. He was just not able to recall. Like with most families, there are just some things that are hard for us to believe they could ever totally forget.

We understand when they can't quickly recall names or details, but we still tend to think we can do something to help them remember people and events of personal importance. And when they still can't recall, it is heartbreaking. So, being the dutiful, determined caregivers that we are, we search for another way to assist them in retrieving this information that we know is still up there, hidden away in their damaged brain.

The creation of a Life Story Book can be just the ticket. For many families, it has proven to be one of the best ways to help preserve and retrieve memories as well as maintain language skills. These books vary every bit as much as people do. Each book is unique to the author, the individual telling his or her story as well as the creator, the person tasked with documenting the overall project. From my experience the best books are created by either certified speech and language pathologists (SLP) or by graduate students in a SLP program that offers clinical experience within a dementia care setting.

With the right direction and guidelines, these books can also be created by a special friend, family member or a health care employee. Often, they are not quite as effective, but nevertheless something is always better than nothing. My only word of caution is that when someone knows the "author" of the story, there is a tendency to correct details, such as people's names, dates, or places. The pitfall occurs when others don't recognize that the ownership of this book belongs solely to the person who is telling his or her story and their own memories.

The key to a successful Life Story Book is that it is told in their "voice" using **their** words and language. Expressing concerns or attempts to ensure proper grammar and accuracy can sabotage the entire project. Once when a grandson was trying to interview his grandfather, his grandmother kept interrupting. She wanted so badly to be helpful and was sweetly, quietly editing her husband's remarks.

Abruptly, his grandfather stood up. "Ask her. She knows everything!" he said. Then he walked out of the room.

As with so many other things in life, timing is everything. When the book is created while a person is in the early middle stage of dementia, it can be a source of pride — "This is who I am." The collaboration and development of this book confirms identity and a sense of self. And, as the disease progresses, these feelings are reaffirmed with each retelling of these stories by the author. These life stories can be used socially with family members, friends, or visitors in the home; or used therapeutically by staff in an adult day program, memory care facility, or other healthcare setting.

With some people, if they are approached in the very early stages of the disease, it starts to look and sound more like an autobiography. The author gets entangled with excessive details and chronological order. Then, the outcome is an uncompleted, fragmented novel rather than a collection of interesting stories about that person's life. People with dementia understand the word "failure" even when its unspoken. After a perceived failure, it's difficult effectively to persuade them to try to tackle this project ever again, even at a much later date. The frequent blows dealt to their self-esteem by this disease, chips away at their self-confidence. This holds true of any unsuccessful attempts or feelings of inadequacies they experience. Unpleasant memories often get stuck and are not easily forgotten.

With my dad, I almost waited too late. For several years there was ample opportunity to have his Life Story Book made by one of the SLP students that came to Friends Place for one of their clinical educational trainings. Unfortunately, they began their day at 9:00 am whereas my dad slept-in late every day. He refused to "get up in the middle of the night," as he would say, for anything or anyone. Since I knew that I could create one for him, I never pressed the issue. But as time began to slip away from me, so were his stories slowly, silently being stolen from him.

When I remembered a sign I once saw at an arts and crafts fair,

"*Sure you can make it, but will you,*" the message really hit home. I knew I needed to act quickly and find another course of action or his stories would be gone forever. This would be an enormous loss and an injustice to my dad as well as our entire family. So, I contacted one of the faculty at a local university and arranged to hire a speech and language pathology student to create a Life Story Book for my Dad. That year it was my Christmas gift to him, each of my two sons, and for me.

We all looked through his book, enjoyed the photographs and stories, and then promptly put it away. Once again, I found myself making the same mistake as so many other families. I should have known better, but sometimes I'm nothing more than a daughter; and all my professional knowledge gets lost in time, tasks, and emotions. We had all received a wonderful gift and yet had never really used it, which takes me back to the beginning of this story.

Although I truly regret not doing it sooner, I am thankful that I finally had the good sense to take it off the shelf that day and encourage my dad to read it to my cousin. The two of them were sitting together at the kitchen table while I was preparing dinner. My father had been such a talker his entire life that every time I saw him sitting in silence, my heart filled with sadness.

I sat the book down on the table in front of him and said, "Dad, why don't you read your book to Sheri?" He looked up at me, hesitated, looked at my cousin, and then pushed the book over in front of her. "Here," he said.

I moved the book back over, so it was situated in between them. "Dad, these are <u>your</u> stories. Maybe you could read her just one". As he sat there staring at the first two pages, I wasn't sure what to expect. Then with mix of shyness and uncertainty, he began to read the first story. Then, the next. And the next.

These books can be such vital caregiving tools when families know when and how to use them. All too often families have one of these books made without fully understanding all the benefits. When used properly, they materialize into the perfect gift that keeps on giving - to you, your loved-one, family members and friends. They prompt interesting conversations and rekindle meaningful memories. Additionally, verbally reading the stories will help keep vocal cords strong, minimizing or preventing swallowing difficulties, which often occurs in the late stages of Alzheimer's.

After that, I began using his Life Story Book on a regular basis. For as long as my dad was able, I would bring him over to the house twice a week for dinner and a very modified game of dominoes. Since he no longer had any interest in television and was frequently limited to only vague social conversations, his book continued to bring both of us great joy and entertainment. On those days, rather than sitting in silence while he waited for me to finish up dinner, he would read a couple of his stories out loud to me. For much of the remainder of those evenings as well as on the drive back to his memory care facility, the essence of one of the stories read earlier became a theme in his thoughts and conversations.

One evening when he was reading his book, he turned the page and just stopped. He was staring intently at a photograph of him and my mother, taken at a nightclub on their first wedding anniversary. He looked and sounded confused as he said, "I don't know who this is." Even as I explained, his expression never changed. Finally, he read the story on the opposite page about when he first met my mom and started dating her. When he finished, he smiled and said, "She sure was pretty. I was crazy about her." He forgot her name, forgot who she was, but in that moment, he remembered her. My mother was the love of his life and his wife for almost 61 years.

People always say to be careful what you wish for. There was a time when my dad was first living with me that he seemed to talk non-stop. This wasn't anything new for him; he always loved to talk to anyone, at any time. But it was a huge adjustment for me. I was used to being by myself with long periods of silence, which I thoroughly enjoyed. Sometimes he made me a little crazy. Actually, back then he managed to unwittingly drive me berserk pretty often, as he was constantly by my side, accompanying me practically everywhere I went. His conversations began upon waking and seemed to end only when he was sleeping.

Then we came to that time when I would have given most anything to have a do-over, a second chance to have him drive me a wee bit insane. Most of his words were gone and his reading skills diminished to a point that it was a struggle to even read a sentence or two. A two-way conversation was rare, even impossible on some days during his last few months. But at least I still had his memories and could hear his language with his words preserved in his Life Story book. As I began reading his stories back to him, I could cherish these stories, hearing his voice as I read each word out loud. Sometimes, pretending things were still the way they used to be and my 'ole dad was fully back with me in that moment, I would begin each story by saying, "Boy, wait until you hear this one!"

With my dad's Life Story Book, "***Charley's Adventures***," our family will forever have this great blessing and continued enjoyment of so many of his favorite tales all told by him ...in his own words.

"Memory is the diary that we all carry with us."
—Oscar Wilde

Chapter 12

A Life of Worthy Endeavors

Robert was both the first person to attend Friends Place and the only member there on opening day. I've always thought he was the perfect person to have embedded forever in my mind with all the other memories, excitement, and utter confusion on the first day of a brand-new business. His impeccable manners and abundant expressions of gratitude carried us through that day.

On that first morning, Robert showed up looking as sharp as he did every day thereafter. He was dressed in slacks, a sport coat, and the greatest looking cowboy dress hat that I had ever seen. As soon as he came in the door, he removed his hat and placed it on the very top of the armoire where it remained until time to leave at the end of the day. Even now, I'm not sure if it was the hat that was so impressive or solely the image created by the man that was wearing it. He was truly a person of dignity.

I've found that the easiest way to describe Robert has been to say that if you could look up "genuine Texas gentleman" in the encyclopedia or dictionary, you would see a photograph of Robert. He was someone whom you felt should be addressed as "Mister," but on that first day he gave us all permission to call him by his first name.

True to his southern upbringing in rural west Texas, where manners are not optional, he was always polite and typically soft-spoken. Robert's faith and his family, his wife and two loving daughters, were the most important things in his world. Following in the footsteps of his father and grandfather, he had served for many years as an Elder in his church.

I had decided long before I opened the center that each day before lunch was served, we would all stand to recite the Pledge of Allegiance to the flag. Then those wanting to participate in the mealtime blessing would remain standing and bow their heads, while one of the members said grace. The first couple of weeks it seemed easier to just have one of the staff do it. Then, with about two dozen members in the dining room, I decided it was time to start asking if one of them would be willing to lead us in prayer.

To me, Robert was the obvious choice to begin this tradition but with his quiet demeanor, some of the staff were doubtful if everyone would be able to hear him. That day he surprised us all as his strong, faithful, and commanding voice as he began the prayer with a resounding "Dear Heavenly Father," which was loud enough for all to hear, and heads remained respectfully bowed until we heard the "Amen." Afterwards, I thanked him for saying such a heartfelt blessing. In response, he thanked me "very kindly" for asking him. This was the first of the many lessons that my staff members learned from those entrusted to us. The essence of a person remains despite the disease.

Respect comes from deep feelings of admiration one has for another based on that person's abilities and achievements. As caregivers we need to be mindful of each person's lifetime roles, whether great or small. Some people's professional lives or lifetime accomplishments are so strongly interwoven into their personal lives that it becomes their identity. It is who they are for the rest of their lives.

When I was growing up, I was taught that we always showed respect to our elders and all others in positions of authority. It didn't matter if we liked them, agreed with their opinions, or if they acted respectful to others. It was just the right thing to do.

Certain professions --like physicians, ministers, teachers, nurses, law enforcement, and attorneys-- are accustomed to being treated with additional layers of respect and courtesies throughout their careers. Also, these are all "helping" occupations so their innate desire to assist others usually doesn't go away when they stop working. Even long after retirement, they will still feel defined by their lifetime role or responsibility.

Consider the personalities or character traits of almost any occupation. You're likely to find that the essence of that position is still within them and continues to be reflected in their actions or demeanors. Salesmen are friendly and like to talk, executives or managers like to be in charge, and engineers like things predictable and exact.

Other vocations define us as well. I know men that pride themselves on their accomplishments as fathers. They consider decades of being the "Coach" and teaching soccer or baseball to sons, daughters, and other kids among their proudest achievements. As they should. A lifetime devoted to scouting, teaching Sunday school to youngsters, volunteering with the American Red Cross, or doing missionary work creates enormous feelings of satisfaction and personal triumphs. Worthy endeavors, such as these, create a strong sense of self-worth and purpose that forever defines that person.

For some women, being a good and loving mother means everything. For them this is the greatest achievement to which they could aspire. And that really doesn't change. Sometimes people talk about role reversal with dementia. But I promise you, it's a huge mistake to think they no longer see themselves in this role. If you think you are going to "mother" your mother, you are in for a big awakening. Never lose sight of the fact that our mothers are always the Mother. Your father is always the Father, a husband is always the head of the household and a wife is pretty much always in charge of almost everything. It matters not if they are still capable of fulfilling the responsibilities which would normally accompany or define that lifetime role. That's just the way it is -- the mother is still the Mother.

My dad was very proud to be a father. He had a real Southern upbringing and was truly a gentleman in every sense of the word. Anyone who has ever had the pleasure of meeting my dad would describe him as friendly, caring, and social. He loved to give compliments, lived to play cards or dominoes, and delighted in doing things for others. His family and friends were always important to him.

There are people who have known my dad for years and have no idea what he did for a living. However, they've probably heard him say more than once that he taught everyone in the family how to drive. His wife, daughter, grandsons and even his great grandson. He's very proud of that, which brings me to another story. This is the lesson I learned firsthand about the significance of lifetime roles - and about patience. Also, it serves as a reminder of how little it takes to make someone feel important and needed.

It first happened when Dad moved in with me shortly after my mother died. This was also the same time that I realized I would seldom be going anywhere again without him accompanying me. We were both still adjusting to new norms and a lot of changes.

It seemed as if every time my dad and I got ready to go somewhere together, the dynamics of our relationship reverted back to my teenage years. The moment I got behind the wheel with him in the car, I was no longer that sixty-something, independent woman. Suddenly, I was once again that fifteen-year-old daughter with her parent/driving instructor in the passenger seat. Every time, with never an exception, I was reminded to check my mirrors and adjust my seat (as if someone else had been driving the car) and to look behind me. He cautioned me at every light and stop sign. I was warned about any approaching car as well as made aware of the speed limit each time we passed a sign. It was very sweet and annoying all at the same time. On days when we were running errands together, it meant getting in and out of the car numerous times, which was even more frustrating as the entire script was repeated again, and again. By the time we arrived home those first few weeks I was trying really hard not to be grumpy but was not always successful.

So, this is how I dealt with his good intentions and was able to give him the respect due to a loving father and concerned driving coach. I knew enough to know that I wasn't going to change his behavior; therefore, I needed to modify my attitude and response. From then on, I became the dutiful "co-pilot," acknowledging each comment with a "Thank you!" or "CHECK!" It was quick, easy, and painless. Made for a few laughs here and there and allowed him to maintain a sense of purpose. I stopped getting irritable and was able to be the understanding daughter he deserved.

In addition to being personally mindful of the significance of these roles, families need to safeguard that any others involved with providing care or services understand as well. It's a mistake to assume that all healthcare workers have been fully trained in best dementia care practices to the extent of understanding the importance of how they address a patient or client.

Maybe it's because of my age, but it bothers me when someone I don't know calls me "Sweetie" or "Honey." I've lived in the South almost all my life and know it's a common expression, but I still don't like it. Waitresses will often use it as a friendly greeting or to address someone they don't know by name. Paid caregivers working in nursing homes or providing in-home care use it often as a term of endearment. More times than I can count, I have corrected healthcare staff members about the inappropriateness of calling everyone "Sweetie." One woman told me that she didn't see anything wrong with saying that because she was just being nice and that's how she always talks. Although she thought it was fine, I fervently thought it was disrespectful. So, I asked her, "Do you call your doctor or your pastor at your church "Sweetie?" I'm sure you can envision the look she gave me.

In their defense, the vast majority of paid caregivers do this type of work for only one reason; they genuinely care about others. Again,

I believe it all goes back to training of acceptable practices. It is both polite as well as appropriate for any person assisting an adult to give them full respect.

Many times, I've had a family member tell me, as an administrative staff, how their loved one would prefer to be addressed, only to get a different response when I would personally ask him or her. This tale of a former resident (name changed) illustrates exactly what I mean. When Dr. William Martin's daughter was admitting him, she told me the staff could call him Billy. "That's what he likes and what all of his friends call him," she said. However, when I posed the question to him, he said I could call him Bill. When the nurse asked him, she was told that he would prefer her to call him William. And when any of the younger nurse's aides or other staff inquired, he informed each one that "Dr. Martin, would be fine."

All caregivers need to understand that they are not taking care of a dementia patient. Rather, they are assisting or providing care and services to an adult, a person deserving of respect who is living with memory problems and cognitive impairment.

Dignity is associated with many words such as "worthiness," "honor," "importance," "self-respect," "significance," "distinction," "greatness," and "status." A person of "dignity" is considered someone of an honorable rank, position, or distinction because of the noteworthy way they lived their life.

Anyone who has the honor of being a caregiver also has the privilege of knowing and caring for someone of importance. We become the keepers and protectors of the memories of their lifetime roles as we travel with them on this new journey to ensure their dignity remains.

> "Dignity does not consist in possessing honors, but in deserving them."
> —Aristotle

Chapter 13

What If It Were So?

I am not even a little ashamed to tell you that I can tell a lie better than almost anybody in the world. Countless families will tell you the same thing. Just as many will likely brag about how they have learned from me the essential ins and outs of convincingly telling untruths to others. But that was not how I was reared.

Even today, I still vividly recall an incident from a family road trip one summer when I was probably about six years old. It was sometime in the mid-fifties and we had stopped for gas. It was a scorching hot day and there I was standing in front of a big, red Coca-Cola® vending machine. It seemed to me almost unimaginable that for five cents, you could purchase a cold bottle of soda, right then and there, while you were outside in the parking lot. Then I saw the nickel in the coin return.

Completely lost in thought, I never noticed that my father had walked up behind me until I reached for the coin. Suddenly, I heard his strong and serious voice. "That's not yours," he said. Then, he instructed me to go inside and return the nickel to the service station operator.

That was just one of many lessons throughout my childhood which my dad taught me about virtues and honesty. From him, I also learned the importance of integrity, good morals, loyalty, and faithfulness. Now, some sixty years later, here I am frequently telling my dad little white lies, filling an entire chapter with a different perspective on truthfulness, and proclaiming the benefits of making false statements.

In my "real" life, I am a very honest person. But when we are caring for a person with any type of dementia, our focus should be on the outcomes rather than the truth. Promising to tell the truth, the whole truth and nothing but the truth is absolutely appropriate and correct in a courtroom, but it is seldom the best practice in the world of dementia.

Many people think it is always wrong to tell a lie. Also, they believe that a lie is different than a fib. Since technically any false statement is a "lie," few people can truthfully say they have never lied to someone at some time. How honest are most, when asked, "Do these jeans make me look fat?" And, what would you say if someone asked your opinion about their selection of paint, while you were gazing at an entire room which had just been repainted? Surely, you would not be brutally honest, even if you thought it was a beastly color.

We use little white lies because it makes others feel better than if we were candid. And yet, family caregivers are inclined to think they should adopt a different code of conduct when they assume the responsibility for care of a loved-one. In the beginning, they tend to keep details accurate, statements factual, and correct any deviations from reality.

When the suggestion of lying to a spouse, parent, or partner first comes up in a support group or during any other discussion with a caregiver, there is always a dilemma. Most have strong opinions with a fixed sense of righteousness. Seldom are any of them on the fence. Spouses will often say with great certainty that they have never lied to their wives or husbands, while also making it crystal clear that they never will. Never, as in no exceptions. Some adult children feel that it would be a dishonor to lie to their parent but are more likely to stretch the truth than are spouses.

Is honesty really the best policy when caring for someone with Alzheimer's or dementia? Is the truth more important than the outcomes? What is the truth? These might seem to be easy questions but not if the one you love hallucinates or is delusional. While these symptoms are not uncommon with Alzheimer's disease, people with Lewy Body Dementia (LBD) experience frequent hallucinations that are much more vivid and often reoccurring. Seldom can they be ignored or easily dismissed. When these disturbing visions or delusional thoughts begin to cause extreme anxiety and frustrations for them and for you on a regular basis, moral views of truth and honesty will quickly change.

When a person with dementia hallucinates or has delusions, their reality is quite different than ours, and the facts are blurred. In order to speak the truth, we need to be in accordance with the same facts or ideas. Whose reality is going to be accepted, theirs or ours? With hallucinations or delusional thinking, these are not one and the same. Seldom, close to never, will they accept our view. The truth will be perceived as a lie and honesty is more likely to increase anger and frustration rather than be calming and reassuring. Only when a shared reality is acknowledged, are we seemingly able to speak honestly and truthfully.

Rarely are hallucinations pleasant or easy to ignore. When we dream at nighttime, we don't stop to question any of the facts in the story that our brain is creating but instead accept things at face value. The next morning, just like with many of our own bad dreams, it can be hard to explain the details of what happened. Things, places, and people don't completely make sense and are not as they should be. Sometimes hallucinations can be the same way. They resemble a horrid nightmare that is occurring in the daytime while one is fully awake. Often with Lewy Body dementia, dreams can continue and get acted out when loved ones get out of bed as they do not always fully awake from the dream state. Some families have described it as being almost like a fantasy nightmare, in which they are walking and talking while still asleep and have momentarily lost touch with the real world.

Animals and children are common themes of hallucinations with LBD, sometimes both being seen together. Seldom are these like cute little stories with happy endings. Rather, imagine looking out your family room window. You see and hear a yard full of young children innocently playing while only a few feet away the swimming pool has become infested with ferocious looking alligators. How frightening it must be, seeing all of this with your own eyes and knowing the potential danger to these children. When you try to get help, someone else walks over, looks out, and calmly says, "There's nothing there." But you know differently and must react quickly. There is no time to argue with this senseless person. How can they not see what you are seeing right before your eyes?

Frequently, at least in the beginning, there is a tendency for caregivers to try to convince the person that this is merely a hallucination, that none of this is real. Again, what if this were ***you*** and ***your*** vision? You would probably be yelling at the top of your lungs all the while panicking about the safety of these children and at the absurdity that someone thinks this is "just" in our minds. Of course, we would know it is real. We have seen it! We have heard it! Now we are mad, upset and react! Undoubtedly not in a calm and positive way.

With almost any type of hallucination or delusional behavior, we need first to step back from <u>our</u> reality and address the circumstances with a different point of view. One effective way to approach these non-existing situations is to ask ourselves, "What if it were so?" It is only then, that we might be able to respond appropriately.

So, what if this scenario were true. What would you, as a bystander do in that instance? For me personally and without a doubt, I know that a pool filled with alligators is not something that I would ever want to tackle on my own. Nor is it likely I would be able to get all the kids safely out of the yard without creating sheer panic.

This becomes one of those many times, in the world of dementia, when we realize that the telephone becomes our lifeline. If it were so, I would call the police, report the situation, and request immediate help. Now, in order to resolve this problem, we need to appear to respond in the same way by recreating the same actions. Pick up the phone, pretend to call the police within earshot of your loved-one, and with the sincerest of emotions as if responding to a dreadful situation, make your "report."

When it comes to dealing with delusions or hallucinations, phony phone calls can be almost as good as having a best friend by your side. Fake calls can made for a variety of reasons. You can call animal control to get the elephants out of the yard or the tigers out of the tree. You can call the police to have them evacuate the 20 or 30 people that are in your living room refusing to leave or the excessive number of unattended children in the den. You can call your son and demand that he brings back the truck he "stole" from his father before you call the sheriff. They are effective because they show that we are taking their problem or concern seriously and we are willing to take an action to correct it.

Perhaps you have already gone through the ordeal of trying to locate their missing personal belongings. Let me assure you that with this disease nothing is ever misplaced or temporarily lost. In their minds, with the utmost certainty, these items have been stolen. Yet another good reason for a bogus call to the local authorities to inform them of the theft of their missing purse, leather jacket, wallet, cash, or checkbook. After you've made the report, then you can peacefully look for these items alone in an inconspicuous manner.

Seldom are we lucky enough to do and say the right thing the first time. Like so many new habits and routines in our lives, we must practice a new norm. Sadly, many times these same visions or delusional thoughts can recur numerous times. We then need to figure out an effective script in our mind that works, rehearse it, and stick with it. It can be used until the day it is no longer necessary or when a different one needs to be conceived.

Most of us would easily agree that there is a huge difference between saying a little white lie versus telling a big whopper of a story. A fib is usually a trivial falsity about something unimportant whereas we tend to think of a lie as a fabrication being told for a personal gain, with the explicit intention of being deceitful and deceptive.

Through the years, many different terms have been used to refer to a more compassionate type of communication dealing with untruths. Caregivers will often use therapeutic lies as an act of kindness, not with the intent of being devious. In support groups, families have often shared with others the many benefits of learning how to speak "Fibberish." This is a term created by a caring wife to best describe a language of loving deceptions. It is important to understand that if they see it, hear it, think it –then it is real. At the very least, we must acknowledge that it is real to them which is all that matters. And the facts as we know them will not work in a delusional world of fantasy.

Experience has taught me that there is a time and place to be completely honest. Sometimes it is purely about love and compassion whereas other times, caregivers are just trying to keep the peace. But all caregivers must know, or figure out quickly, when it is the right time to "lie" and the best time to be honest. There really are times and places for lies, stretching the truth, omissions of facts, and telling tall tales.

It's like anytime an older person is looking for their mother. Do you want to take the wind from their sails with the truth or gently guide them toward the shore? Some comments and behaviors are windows into their hearts that allow us to deal with their honest emotions and feelings. This longing has nothing to do with hallucinations or delusions but with sad emotions or loneliness. People tend to make this question more complicated than it needs to be. "Have you seen my mother?" The easy, honest answer is "No." A caring person should then ask back, "Why are you looking for her?" When we listen fully to the emotions of the words, we are able to reply in a manner which is most appropriate for that individual.

To this day my heart still breaks recalling a conversation with a salesclerk when she found out I worked with people with dementia. She was telling me that her husband's grandmother had Alzheimer's and how sad it was because the woman was frequently asking for her mother. Each time they would explain to her that her mother was dead, and she would start crying and get so upset asking why no one told her. Apparently, this happened over and over with his grandmother grieving each time. I was shocked. I can never understand how anyone might think that this was a good idea when it continues to have such a miserable outcome. Some families still think if they tell a loved one often enough, that they might remember. While, quite frankly, others are too uncomfortable or uncertain how to respond.

This question is a perfect example of a time that you don't need to decide between the truth or a lie. I've probably addressed this at least a thousand times in my career. It seems obvious to me and comes first to my mind that no one would ever be looking for someone whom they knew to be deceased. It's good common sense, even for one with dementia. Maybe it's because I am a woman, but I know that regardless of how tough or independent we might be, when something goes wrong, we want our mothers. That's the plain and simple truth. We want to see them or talk to them because they were always the one that could kiss a boo-boo, wipe a tear, walk with us in troubled times, and make everything better.

I will look them in the face and tell them with the utmost honesty that I have not seen their mother. It's a good assumption that they are looking for their mother because of missing her or feeling all alone. Often, they just need someone to be with them, so I sit down, and we talk about all ways that mothers are special. That is the only truth needed. Then, sometimes we talk about how we miss them. Death is something that I prefer to neither confirm nor deny. I believe it is more compassionate to let them reach their own conclusions, at their own time, whatever that may be. Death is often a deep and painful memory. The realization of someone you love being dead is seldom pleasant but listening with our hearts can truly be comforting and consoling.

There was a lady with vascular dementia living in the memory care community at an assisted living facility, who despite her memory problems, was oriented almost all the time. Before her mother's death, she and her mother had lived together most of their lives. With great love she often shared the details of her mother's "final resting place." She described the beauty of the spot as being on the top of a grassy hill under a large shade tree with a stunning view. It was important to her and she talked about it frequently. So, the staff were caught completely off guard one day when she was near hysterics trying to get off the unit to meet her mother downstairs. As their efforts to redirect her or prevent her from getting on the elevators intensified, the more distraught she became. I was called to the unit to see if I could help.

Keeping her there was not working so I suggested that we go downstairs together, and I would wait with her until her mother came. This brought immediate relief. We often visited so it wasn't unusual for me to be there with her. As we sat talking about her mother, I made a casual comment that I must have gotten mixed up. "For some reason," I said, "I thought I remembered your telling me something about this special beautiful site up on the top of a hill where I thought you told me one time that your mother was buried there." I posed the statement like a question and I could see her thinking hard about what I had said. Then, after a moment, I added, "Was there an enormous shade tree there?"

Slowly moving her head to indicate the affirmative, I could see both sadness and joy on her face as her memories were retrieved. We sat a while longer talking about how much she must have loved her mother to have found such a spectacular place for her. A short while later, she willingly returned with me to go back upstairs for dinner, embracing, once again, lovely recollections of her mother.

Then there was George and his dog. As George sat each day in his wheelchair, his faithful companion was by his side. Ever since the dog showed up, he was happier and calmer, petting and talking to this beloved animal throughout the day. There was some concern among a few of the staff at the nursing home about this dog. Only George could see the dog. It wasn't real. What about reality orientation? Would it be dishonest to pretend like it was there? It was decided that true joy and happiness is good for the body, mind, and soul — regardless of the source. The dog stayed.

As a loving daughter, I fibbed to my father to alleviate his concerns and put his mind at ease. Like so many other men attending day programs or living in memory care communities, he perceived all the social activities and gatherings as being work related – his job. He started to worry about his finances and discreetly shared with me that they had not been paying him. So, I told him that the money he got paid for "working" at his new place was directly deposited into his banking account. Plus, he was now making so much money at this new job, that all his living expenses were covered. He said he sure was relieved because this was the best job he had ever had and didn't know how he should handle the situation. Naturally, this made-up story had a happy ending.

It took a while for me to be able to lie, even casually, to my dad about anything. Like a lot of other caregivers, I tried to keep us both on the same path to reality. It's such a conundrum how they can remember some things and not others, how their abilities come and go from one day to the next, especially for someone like my dad with vascular dementia. I think it's hard for many of us to accept that they are not going to be able to do any better than they can do that day, at that time. Tomorrow might be different

For over a year when he was first living in memory care, he would call me every day at 4:30pm. What a gift that was for both of us to be able to connect each and every day. Regardless of where I might be physically, I was able to be "present" for him at the other end of the line. Then as the disease progressed, I could tell by his tone of voice that he was rarely speaking to his daughter but rather just talking to the person at the other end. "Oh, good I got you," he would say, "so you'll make the calls and take care of everything?" Every day the conversation was the same with absolutely no variance on his part.

There were days that I couldn't seem to resist the temptation to bring him back and would ask stupid things like, who did he think he was speaking to or who was I supposed to be calling. He answered consistently saying "I'm calling… **you!**" and that I was supposed to be calling "**them.**" Once (only once) I asked why I am calling "them," only to be told with great disappointment in his voice, "Never mind".

It was then that I realized that these phone calls were no longer a connective bridge between father and daughter but rather an extension of his "work" day. Even though I continued to call him Dad when I answered, he was too focused on this one final task of his day to realize that this was not a usual response from a secretary. Each day I would assure him that I would make the calls and take care of everything. Hearing the elation in his voice, as he would say "Wonderful!" made the entire charade worthwhile and seemed to merit a little fib.

When we are caring for a loved-one with dementia, it truly doesn't matter who is right or wrong. Again, truth matters less than the outcomes. What counts the most is the way our compassionate responses can make them feel safe, satisfied, and reassured. I will tell you honestly that I loved fibbing to my dad because these little lies enabled him to be worry-free, happy, and content.

> **"Kindness enriches our life; with kindness mysterious things become clear, difficult things become easy, and dull things become cheerful."**
> **— Leo Tolstoy**

Chapter 14

Home is Where the Heart Is

It was a simple but nice dinner. Irene had made one of Bert's favorites and they both talked more than usual. He was in an especially good mood that evening, almost romantic. Since he had spent the day enjoying being at an adult day program, which also gave her a break, both of their dispositions were better than usual. As best he could, Bert even helped her clear the dishes and was very attentive.

Afterwards, he even seemed to enjoy watching television with her just like they used to do. Irene knew that this was an unusual occasion. Although married almost sixty years, much had changed since he was first diagnosed with Alzheimer's about eight years ago. Now she had learned to appreciate the few sporadic times when things seemed almost normal. This night was one of those rare occurrences.

When the show ended, he looked at her sweetly and in almost a bashful tone said, "Well, this was nice, but I need to get home now."

I wish I could tell you that this seldom happens, but I can't. It happens more than you can imagine and usually without warning. Just like so many other behaviors commonly associated with dementia, you might never experience this situation. If you do, you'll be able to handle it better if you're already primed for the possibility.

Earl, a devoted husband, and caregiver wore himself out every evening after supper touring his wife around their home of over fifty plus years. In an attempt to convince her that this *was* her home, he showed her family photographs on the walls, treasured items accumulated during their long life together, her personal clothes, and belongings in their bedroom. She acknowledged everything with hints of recognition. Then, when they finished making the rounds of their home, would pleadingly ask him once again, "Can I go home now?"

Some families have even gone to extremes at times to help take them to "this" place they call home. Janet planned an arduous two-day road trip to drive Jim back to his childhood home in Ohio. He had recently been talking repeatedly about wanting to go home so she assumed he was expressing his need to see his brothers and visit his hometown. It was a difficult journey for both of them. They were riding in the car for long periods of time, driving lengthy stretches of highway, taking frequent restroom stops, eating in restaurants, and staying overnight in a hotel. Within hours of their arrival at their final destination, he was anxious and uncomfortable. Jim said he was ready to go "home."

Every caregiver is going to cope better with a new situation if he or she is already mentally prepared and has given previous thought to how they might best respond. Telling and showing them that this is their home is just not going to work. Believe me, absolutely hundreds of families have already tried that before you, all to no avail. Now consider this. Right this very minute could someone – anyone - convince you that your home was NOT your home. Of course not. We would think they were either stupid or utterly ridiculous to even suggest that we don't know our own home.

Trying to convince someone with dementia of anything different than what they know (not think but know) to be true is only going to result in frustration and anger …probably for both of you. Their reality is seldom the same as ours. When we step back and ask ourselves the ever-powerful question, "What if it were so?" we will be much more likely to discern a plausible and reassuring response.

But, don't just say those words. Seriously ponder that possibility. Then, accept this revised version of the "truth" and respond or react according to these newly acquired facts. What if this wasn't her house? Why would she be there? What if it wasn't your house? Why would you be there?

Begin with simple. It's always going to be better. "We're spending the night here and we'll go home in the morning." And why might you do that? Oh, it might be because we were invited to stay over... it's pretty late to drive home tonight... they're spraying the house for bugs... or they're painting the house and the fumes are too strong to stay there. With time, you can think of other possibilities as well, regarding why you might not be going home tonight.

That might be all you need to resolve the issue for that one night, for a few days or weeks. Just like everything else with this disease, it doesn't always work; and if it works once, it might not work all the time. This is one of those rare, exceptional times when you hope their short-term memory problems prevail so that they don't wake up the next morning saying, "Great! Are we ready to head back home now?"

Should this happen, take a deep breath, smile, and begin again using redirection based on the what-if-it-were-so approach. My guess is that if you were going somewhere first thing in the morning, you would want to have something to eat before starting out. Over breakfast the discussion might be about the weather or planning for the day ahead. Ask how they would like to spend their day. Do they have any suggestions for something fun to do together? If it's a nice day, the two of you might enjoy just taking a drive somewhere. Just keep talking and taking baby steps of conversation until you can move your loved one from one restless thought to a more favorable, peaceful one.

Let's imagine for a minute that this was so. It was not their house, and their real "home" was not simply another house nearby. Say it's in another city or another state; then that would involve taking a trip to get there. Together you could begin to work on travel plans, making a list of all the tasks that would need to be handled in addition to decisions which would need to be made. Would you drive or fly? Should you make hotel reservations? What about the mail and the newspaper? Is there a dog or cat that will need to be cared for? The list goes on and on. It might take several hours, perhaps even days to finalize all these details.

Just like any other trip you might plan, consider all the facts –the weather, the cost, the logistics. Perhaps it is too hot, too cold, too pricey, too overwhelming to even think about going right now. You might both decide that it would be wise to stop for a while and take a breather from all this exhausting trip preparation. When you do take a nice little break, don't bring it back up for discussion unless they do. Then begin again.

Families become very befuddled trying to figure out where is this place called "home." When a person with dementia starts talking about going home, seldom is it even a real place, an actual residence or dwelling which they are seeking. In the realm of dementia, "home" is that place where everything is familiar, where we feel comfortable, and where we know that we are safe and secure. Maybe that's why we so often hear, "Home is where the heart is." It's an emotional place in our mind that allows us to feel loved, peaceful and that all is right with the world –our world. It is not a place we can drive them to, but we might be able to transport them there with sincere understanding and loving, reassuring words.

There was a time in the beginning when I was having trouble adjusting to my dad's living with me. It had been a year filled with heartache, changes, and challenges. Within less than twelve months' time, my mother had died, dad had moved to Dallas to live with me, and my childhood sweetheart and husband of 43 years had died. It was still the same house but so many things were different. On those especially difficult days, I would wish that my life could be the way it used to be. I wanted to be like Dorothy in the Wizard of Oz, and just click my heels together 3 times, saying "There's no place like home," and find myself back at the "home" I remembered and coveted. There is no other place like our home.

"Where we love is home, home that our feet may leave, but not our hearts."
—**Oliver Wendell Holmes, Sr.**

Chapter 15

Superheroes

First, some basic truths about family caregivers. The very best caregivers lose their patience, get frustrated, and make mistakes, sometimes within just hours of getting up in the morning. Some days are easier than others. And when you become a caregiver, either by choice or destiny, you do not get a Superman or Wonder Woman cape. Yep, you're pretty much on your own. You have no superpowers. But don't despair because with a little time, knowledge, support, compassion, and a bit of humor, you can become an authentic, real-life Superhero.

I've seen enough of the Marvel movies with my husband and grandson to know that even superheroes are not perfect. They're good at fighting crime and injustice but they still make mistakes. Just as they are not without a few flaws, it's the same for caregivers. There is no such thing as a perfect caregiver. But rest assured there are plenty of nearly perfect caregivers, and you can certainly be one of those.

Probably all of us have encountered some well-meaning friends or family members during this journey that think they know all the answers and are keen to share what we could or should do differently. However, I would be willing to bet that none of these people are taking care of a loved one with dementia. So, trust me on this, if any of them were genuinely a full-time family caregiver, they would also have their fair share of imperfections. Being human, caring for a person to whom you are related, and dealing with daily challenges seven days a week – 24 hours a day – makes perfection impossible. We must give ourselves permission to make mistakes, credit for trying to do our best, and recognition for being perfect some of the time, maybe even most of the time.

Heroes are admired for their bravery, great deeds, and noteworthy qualities. They can only save the day if they are willing and able to show-up. Personally, I think just about every caregiver I've ever met is a hero, a true champion. However, all caregivers and heroes must be up to the task. They can only accomplish great deeds when they put their own well-being first. It's not selfish; it's survival.

Each of us needs to accept that caring for oneself is a necessity to continue to care for our loved one. This is so critical for all of us to understand. Let me say it again. Caregivers **must** take the time to play, pray, be pampered, or relax for several reasons. It is important for our own health, sense of well-being, and personal happiness. But also, because if we don't, then someone else is going to be taking care of our loved-one and, most likely, it will not be in their own home.

Stress affects all of us. It's just something that most people consider to be just part of life. Some deal with stress better than others, and each of us in our own way. But chronic stress, like the stress related to the pressures of being a family caregiver, can have serious consequences.

Families frequently underestimate the weight of the emotional stress of caring for someone with dementia. When physical care becomes necessary, caregivers tend to be slightly more aware of the impact stress is having on their lives. And yet they still try to carry the burden alone.

Humor me for just a minute. I want you to do a little exercise for me. To appreciate the full weight of stress, I want to start by discussing the weight of a feather. I'm just talking about one tiny feather, like you might find in a pillow. Take a minute and really think about this feather. How much do you think a single feather would weigh?

Visualize placing that one, small feather in your hand. It might seem so insubstantial as to be immeasurable. It shouldn't be difficult to hold it in your hand, palm up, and arm extended for several minutes. Please go ahead and try it right now. Raise your right hand up to about shoulder level and retain that position for at least five minutes. Now, what if you continued to cradle this imaginary feather in your hand, unsupported, for an hour or a day or a week or a month? What seemed weightless at first soon becomes too heavy to grasp. Stress related to caring for a loved one is just like that, too. It becomes more than one can endure.

According to The Family Caregiver Alliance, 30-40% of dementia caregivers suffer from depression and emotional distress. Other effects of stress on a caregiver's mental and emotional health include decrease in quality of life indicators, greater risk for cognitive decline, and increased feelings of anger and irritability. Stress can cause caregivers to start having memory problems, too. Families often jest about this disease being contagious. It's no joke, stress will mess with your mind and your moods.

Family caregivers can also experience significant changes in their physical health. Some common health concerns include digestive problems, frequent headaches, and a greater propensity of viral infections. Chronic stress can also increase the risk of heart disease, diabetes, as well as other serious medical problems.

We all know this, and yet way too many caregivers do not give stress the serious attention it deserves. They fail to connect the dots. It's like a crazy caregiving paradox. They are too busy taking care of their loved one to take care of themselves, but because they don't put their health and general well-being first, they reach a point that they can't take care of them at all. Seriously, does that make any sense when you stop and look at it that way? No, of course not.

Dementia family caregivers think they will be the exception.

After all these years, I still don't know if it's because they think they can walk on water or that they just like being martyrs and are willing to lay down their lives for this debilitating, progressive disease. Most often I see this is the situation when spouses are caring for their wives or husbands. It is a heartbreaking situation for adult children, fearful of losing both their parents; and unfortunately, that happens.

Recently, I heard about a caregiver that finally moved his beloved wife into a memory care facility after years of urging from his concerned children. The next day he died of a heart attack. I wish I could tell you that this was a rare occurrence.

Many years ago, the subject of placement came up at a support group meeting that I facilitated at a local nursing and rehab facility. About half of those attending were still caring for family members at home. At this particular meeting, several asked that all important question, "When did you know it was time?"

It wasn't so much the responses that surprised me as it was hearing basically the same answers from so many. Even with all my years of experience, the commentaries that evening were shocking.

Five husbands spoke first. In every instance, they began by saying that it wasn't their decision. Mostly it was their sons or daughters who lovingly placed their mothers. One by one they told their personal stories. Each husband explained it had happened while he had been in the hospital recovering from a serious medical condition - a bleeding ulcer, heart attack, stroke, nervous breakdown, or pneumonia. Alzheimer's, probably because of the long duration of this disease, is especially notorious for taking two victims at a time.

A daughter in the group quickly added that she too, had been forced to make that agonizing decision to put her mother in a nursing home. Tearfully she said that she worked full time and had several children still at home. When her father died suddenly, she had instantaneously become her mother's primary caregiver. She was divorced with no siblings to help. It broke her heart, but she didn't feel as though she had any other choice.

Another time a woman shared that she and her sister had moved their mother into a memory care community the same night as their father was taken to the intensive care unit following a massive stroke. She added that they were thankful that he had made previous arrangements months before with this facility as a "Plan B." His careful planning made it possible for both of his daughters to be at his bedside while knowing that their mother was receiving the appropriate care that she needed.

Be sure that your "Plan A" includes making ***your*** emotional and physical health a priority. Begin today and make a resolution to do at least one of the "Survival Tips" listed below. People always say they don't have time, but if you truly want to keep a loved one at home as long as possible, you simply must make the time and put your needs first. Most importantly, do these things for you and your own self-preservation. Know that you are a special and unique individual. Have you thought about what your loved one would do without you? Who would step-up to take care of him or her? That alone should be enough for you to realize, you are important, and you do matter. There's probably a lot of other people in your life that also love and care about you and to whom you matter.

We can begin with baby steps but need to stop just thinking about our health and start doing something about it now…today. These "Survival Tips" will reduce or prevent some of the adverse effects of stress. Read through these tips, pick one which appeals to you, and do it. Then, gradually add another until you're doing all of them. For those overachievers, feel free to jump in and start all of them at once. Putting ourselves first is new to many of us but it is not selfish, it is smart. This is how real superhero caregivers successfully navigate the treacherous journey of dementia and survive.

Caregiver Survival Tips

1. **Set aside at least 15 minutes (or longer) each day to do something just for you.** Enjoy a nice cup of tea, meditate,

quietly read a devotional, browse through a magazine, call a friend, or write in a journal. Select a time of day when you can enjoy the activity with limited or no interruptions. You might even have to get up early, stay up late or schedule a time when your loved one is gone or busy.

Maybe once a month or so, you could even take some extra time to go have a massage, take a relaxing bubble bath, have a long lunch with friends or go to a movie that <u>you</u> want to see and eat *all* the popcorn by yourself.

2. **Arrange for some help on a regular basis.** Maybe this 2nd survival tip is exactly what some of us might need to do to consistently accomplish the 1st survival tip on a daily basis. What chore would we most enjoy giving up? Arrange for assistance with cleaning, meals, other household chores, organizing or caregiving tasks. Hire or arrange for a family member or friend to "share the care" for a few hours at least once a month to give us a little free time on the weekend, especially for those still working outside of the home. For a couple of afternoons each week, utilize an adult day program or hire an in-home care companion to allow you to have some "time-out" to re-energize.

For all the women caregivers who think you need to prepare a nice dinner every night to be good wives and good daughters, I give you permission to turn in your apron and take the night off at least once a week (more often is okay, too). Instead of cooking get help with dinner by eating out, getting a take-out meal, or even having pizza or Chinese food delivered. You are still being a good wife or daughter but now, once a week, you might also be happier, calmer, and a little more relaxed.

I remember visiting an older couple in their home and opening the freezer to see nothing but stacks of healthy-style frozen dinners. He was the full-time caregiver for his wife and had been doing everything on his own. When he saw the expression on my face, he kind of smiled and blushed at the same time explaining that he had finally decided he needed help with meals. "No planning, shopping, or cooking ...and clean-up is a breeze!"

3. **Laugh each and every day.** Finding humor and laughing daily is just plain good and healthy for both us and our loved ones! It might be from your situation at hand, your care partner, from a book, friend, or favorite TV show. Is there a funny family story that deserves retelling? What a great time to revive all the old corny knock-knock jokes. If this has not been part of your everyday routine, it should be. Let the laughter begin!

4. **Each day give yourself generous praises.** Make it a habit to give yourself credit. Each morning when you look in the mirror, give yourself a little salute, a "hear-hear" or a pat on the back! Caregivers are all deserving of praise merely for having good intentions and making the effort. You are a giving, loving, devoted caregiver or you wouldn't even be reading this book right now. Remember that each of us can only do the best job we can at any given moment... on any given day. Some days, we might do better than other days, but every day we step up with love and determination to give our loved ones the best possible care.

5. **Exercise on a regular basis.** Just about any form of daily, regular exercise is going to be mentally, physically, and emotionally healthy for both of you. Exercise releases chemicals called endorphins which improve our mood. This is especially helpful to us since caregivers are at a higher risk for depression. Consider a morning stroll around the neighborhood, exercises at the senior center, sittercise in your living room, or going to a fitness center. This might be

the perfect time to begin exploring some of the other stress reducing activities such as yoga, meditation, or tai chi.

Dr. Kenneth Cooper, a Dallas physician who specializes in preventive health and wellness, once stated his belief that everyone would benefit from walking the dog every day, even if they didn't have a dog! Although we have known for a long time 30 minutes a day is the desirable daily goal, he shared that recent studies have shown that it doesn't have to all be done at one time. A person can benefit from 10 minutes of walking, three times a day to achieve the same goal. This story comes to mind anytime I am urging caregivers to find the time to stay physically active. Mostly I share it because I know that caregivers tend to put the needs of others, including their own dogs, before their own health and well-being.

6. **Stay socially connected.** Make time for pleasurable activities and devote time to be with friends. Stay in touch with other family members and friends be it in person, by email or social media. It is essential to be proactive and stay socially connected throughout this journey. Caregivers can easily become victimized by this disease as it progresses, and we find ourselves socially isolated. Ideally, we need to be proactive from the beginning but it's almost never too late to reconnect or even build a new social network. Think about people from church, long-time friends, or neighbors that have tried to reach out to you and get reacquainted. Connections can also be made with other caregivers whom we might meet at support group meetings, neighborhood memory cafés or other social gatherings intended to bring people together that are in similar situations as ours. Often caregivers will find other kindred spirits with whom to share their time enjoying coffee, a cup of tea or a glass of wine together.

For most of us, time is often the biggest obstacle to doing the things we want to do, think we should do, or must do. Caregivers will be the first to tell you that there is never enough time in the day to do what we need to do and certainly no time left for anything else. But I spent my life with the understanding that it is seldom an accurate or acceptable excuse to say, "I don't have time." Since I was young, my dad disciplined me according to his conviction that "There is time to do anything you want to do. It's all about how you set your priorities." Dad believed that if you really "wanted" to do something — truly important to you — you would find the time. And he was right: seize the moment, put on your capes, make time for you, and become a real-life, nearly perfect, Superhero Caregiver!

> **"I think a hero is an ordinary individual who finds strength to persevere and endure in spite of overwhelming obstacles."**
> —Christopher Reeve

Reprinted with permission from the Christopher and Dana Reeve Foundation.

Chapter 16

Me Tarzan. You Jane.

He was focused on my every word, occasionally nodding with a smile reflecting both agreement and understanding. As usual, when I finished my presentation, I asked if anyone had comments or questions. Right away he responded, "Yes! I sure hope my wife was paying attention." He went on to say that she just "doesn't get it," explaining that he is trying to do his best but doesn't always understand what she wants him to do.

Here before me was a person with early stage Alzheimer's sitting next to his wife. She was his care partner and although she started to respond in her own defense, politely chose to let him finish his entire story. Then, she told her side.

It seems that his wife had recently asked him to go get the boxes with the packed-up Christmas decorations from the living room and take all of them to the back bedroom. She was busy in the kitchen and assumed he would take care of this, just as he had always done in past years. But that, of course, was before he started having memory problems.

While two of the boxes had been moved as far as the hallway, the rest remained in their original place in the living room. None of the boxes had made it all the way down the hall to the desired location. When she found him, he was back in the living room, comfortably watching television.

"I thought you were going to put the boxes up for me!" There was a sharp edge to her tone of voice as she stood there with her hands on her hips, glaring at him.

"I did!" he replied. Completely confused by her comment and demeanor, he shrugged his shoulders and casually turned his attention back to the TV program he was viewing.

Upon hearing the recounting of his final words, the room was instantly filled with laughter, shrugs, and more side-to-side they-don't-get-it nods. Apparently, his wife was not the only one there that underestimated the impact Alzheimer's has on language skills. This disease is about much more than being merely forgetful.

They were there with several other couples attending one of the educational sessions of an early stage program. When I was first asked to speak about "Communication," I felt a little apprehensive. I had given countless presentations on this topic to caregivers and I can comfortably talk about almost anything with an individual with the disease. But both conversations were quite different, even if the subject matter was the same. It was the first time that I had spoken about language deficits – or any other symptoms of dementia – in the presence of both "care partners."

For the communication presentation, I usually begin by having everyone do a little quiz. It's called "Think Fast." Each person has a paper with numbered blank lines from one to ten. Before we start, I reassure everyone that no one else will see their answers, we don't grade for spelling, nor do we deduct for poor penmanship. They just need to relax, have fun, and do the best they can.

First, I give them an example by saying, "Name a flower. In the blank, just write down the name of any flower. Easy right? Any questions? Ready to have fun?" Then, I begin. Pretty much as fast as I can, I start blurting out, "Name a famous inventor, a kitchen gadget, something you would blow." I look away, speak a little softer, and continue, "Name a fictional detective, Jewish comedian, exotic fruit...." While I'm speeding through the list of categories, people are asking me to slow down or repeat. I ignore all the requests and avoid any eye contact. This causes reactions that I have fully anticipated.

Those with the disease rarely, if ever, complete the quiz. They will stop writing and put down their pens. Some do it sooner than others. Most will lean back in their chairs with their arms crossed in frustration. Others will just look away into the distance. With Alzheimer's it takes much more time to process spoken language or decode words, so they just give up. For most of them, this unpleasant experience is nothing new. It is an emotional state they encounter every day.

The care partners, those without the disease, tend to have a good time and get totally into the competition. Seldom do they even notice their loved one has stopped participating. As we go over the answers, there's a lot of comments about the things I could have or should have done differently to make it easier. Without the slightest hesitation, they tell me that I was talking too fast, should have paused to give them more time to respond, and my words were not always clearly enunciated.

Now we are getting to the whole point of this exercise. I encourage them to share other tips or techniques that I could have used. They said it would have been helpful if they could have seen the words, rather than just hearing me say them. I should have looked directly at them each time instead of sometimes turning my back to them. And everyone agreed that it would have made a huge difference if the words were repeated or restated until it was clear enough for each of them to understand.

Unknowingly they had stated many of the important skills and guidelines needed to communicate respectfully. This simple exercise reminded them that good communication is indeed a two-way process. It also pointed out that the person sending the message to someone with dementia bears much of the weight of the responsibility for the message to be able to be received according to the other's personal language ability. Once again, we are the ones that need to speak and listen differently if we want successfully to communicate with someone with dementia.

We communicate respectfully with positive words, kind actions and a sensitive awareness of their language skills. It means that we make every effort to say things in a way that we know or hope they can understand. Always talk as an adult to another adult regardless of their limitations. We still use many of the same words but fewer. Our sentences are shorter, and simpler. It might sound a little like a line from an old Tarzan movie, "Me Tarzan. You Jane." Maybe not quite that bare-to-the bones. However, as a good rule of thumb, if a sentence has any if's, and's, or but's, it is probably too long of a sentence.

We speak at a slower pace that allows time for them to process each of our words and give them ample time to respond. If you've ever tried to learn a foreign language, you know that it is much easier to understand written words versus hearing them in a conversation. Even when you master many of the new words and understand simple sentences, if someone else speaks that language fluently and starts talking to you at their normal rate of speech, you're lost after the third or fourth word. Our brain needs time to remember the meaning of each of these words within the context of that conversation.

The same thing happens when a person has dementia. The disease disrupts their ability to have an automatic, almost instant, recall of familiar words as they had before the disease. Words go missing when they are attempting to interpret any spoken language, thus, creating voids in the messages they are receiving. A person needs to be able to understand all the words they hear to respond appropriately. When this happens too often, people with dementia tend to stop responding altogether and will seldom initiate conversations.

Sometimes there are also other good reasons that they don't always respond, which brings to mind another true story. Susan was standing at the sink washing dishes and talking to her husband as he sat behind her at the table. She had asked him an "important" question but received no reply. So, she asked again. Still no response. Finally, she turned to him and spoke a little louder with just a hint of aggravation.

"Can you hear me?" she asked.

"Yep," he said.

"Then, why didn't you answer me?" she asked.

"Didn't know you were talking to me," he said.

"So, just **who** did you think I was talking to?" she asked sarcastically.

"Well …now… I had kind of been wondering about that," he replied innocently.

It would be my guess that this is a similar story that plays out in households across the nation. The point to this amusing story is that we must not assume our loved ones are listening or paying attention to what is being said.

It's easy to think of this disease as being about memory loss and losing sight of the fact that it causes many other problems as well, one of those being attention deficit, making it hard for them to remain focused. Unless we first give them a clue or prompt them in some way to get their attention, it is highly unlikely they will be able to concentrate on any of our words.

In the olden days, there was a town crier ringing his bell to ensure he had the attention of all the local villagers before reading any public announcements or delivering proclamations from the King. About 10 years ago, I realized it would make life easier for both me and my dad if I became sort of like a "town crier," except without the bell or costume.

Even when it was just the two of us and I thought Dad knew I was talking to him; I had to preface my conversation before telling him anything of significance. Otherwise, he would seldom focus on anything I was saying as he was too distracted by his own thoughts or the world around him. By the time he realized I was actually talking to him, he was only able to pick up on a few words and tried to make sense of them out of context.

Once I began using the "town crier" approach, it made a difference for both of us. When there was something important, I wanted or needed him to know, I would look directly at him and say, "Dad, I need you to listen." Only after both of us had made eye contact, I had his full attention, and he understood that my words were meant for him; did I continue our conversation.

Asking our loved ones to give us their attention is both an effective and necessary technique to ensure successful communication. It identifies both the sender of the message as well as the intended receiver. This one little step strengthens remaining language abilities by enabling them to focus on the words in a conversation and respond more appropriately. At least, most of the time.

> **"If you light a lamp for somebody, it will also brighten your path."**
> **—Buddha**

Chapter 17

Sweet Secrets for Success

One evening after supper, Martin went to his wife and asked her to come with him. "I have a little surprise for you," he said. As he opened the bathroom door, he explained that since she had been "working so hard" that day, he thought she would enjoy a nice, quiet bath. A battery-operated candle flickered by the side of the tub, the room was filled with scents of roses and lavender, while music played quietly in the background. He even offered to wash her back, "... like I used to do in the old days," he said. What woman wouldn't be interested in taking a bath under those circumstances? A little romance can go a long way.

Once I was asked if I could give a 30-minute presentation on "Baths and Alzheimer's." I laughed and said I could easily do a day-long seminar because this is such a common challenge for caregivers everywhere. However, the actual bathing process is not nearly as difficult as it is to get a loved one to actually agree to take a bath or a shower in the first place. We must be able to master the power of persuasion or we'll never make it over the first hurdle.

Most caregivers have either personally experienced or been warned by others about the "Battle of the Bath." This can be an enormous challenge in almost any care setting, particularly when dealing with memory loss. There are numerous reasons that people with dementia now resist the idea of taking a shower or bath as opposed to previous years. Most of our loved ones reach the point when they see no need to bathe and have no desire to do so. When they do bathe, it is rarely as often as we think it should be and sooner than our loved ones believe is necessary. Before this disease, most of our loved ones would have bathed daily or very frequently, without a single thought or hesitation. But for most caregivers, those days are gone.

Better to understand our loved ones' current perception of bathing, we need to step into their world and reassess the situation from their viewpoint. Beginning with the what-if-it-were-me approach, I could plausibly envision a number of logical reasons from my perspective for which I might decline should I have dementia. If I believed I just had a shower several hours earlier or maybe last night before I went to bed, I wouldn't see a need for showering again. Perhaps, I would think it unnecessary to shower at all since I hadn't been doing anything to get dirty or to make me sweat. If I were particularly sensitive to changes in temperatures, tended to get cold easily, or was already comfortably (warmly) dressed for the day, I might want to postpone my bath for a while --or another day. If my dear friend had recently fallen in the shower, fractured her hip, and ended up in a nursing home, I would definitely be reluctant. And, if I thought someone were going to try to help me or be in the room with me, I would absolutely refuse. How absurd to think I couldn't do it by myself!

As caregivers, we have a number of options we can exercise when our loved ones show reluctance. We can listen to the reasons they give us (at least today's reason) and respond accordingly. We can ask them directly to share with us the reason that they prefer to refuse. This would entail sitting eye-level and talking with them, since a casual caring conversation is going to be more productive than grilling them. Should our tone of voice be even the tiniest confrontational, their answer will almost certainly be, "because I don't want to." End of story; end of discussion.

As another option, caregivers can just make a wild guess as to why our loved ones don't want to bathe or might be unwilling to discuss it. Maybe they don't know why or can't verbalize their thoughts or apprehensions. Very likely they have good reasons, at least in their minds. Hopefully as loving caregivers we will be motivated to do our best first to understand their concerns and then decide what actions we need to take to overcome those objections.

Our loved ones remain firm in their beliefs that adults take their own showers without any assistance, only when and if they want to. Caregivers can't force them to take a shower and arguing or verbally berating them will almost certainly guarantee steadfast refusal, lasting for days or maybe weeks. Strong emotions tend to create longer lasting memories. Regrettably, they are able to recall quite well some things we hope they might forget. But much to our advantage, loved ones are also able to make pleasurable connections to tasks, people or events.

Ice cream, candy, massages, and favorite songs are just some of the gratifying things which seem to get encoded into our memory banks more easily than others. Throughout my career it has amazed me that regardless of where a person might be within the disease process, they could always seem to locate my office. Although they seldom were able to recall my name, they remembered I had chocolates on my desk. We can use our knowledge of our loved one's personal preferences as leverage to form the same type of association with their daily care. Bribes do work! But the real secret to success with bathing or any other activity of daily living is to view everything from their perspective.

As we prepare to arm ourselves for the battle of the bath, here are some things to consider:
- Some women do not like to get their hair wet in the shower. There might have been a time before the disease, when they preferred to bend over the kitchen sink for shampoos or had weekly appointments at a beauty salon.

- Many healthy minded seniors only bathe 3 – 4 times a week, not daily. Keep in mind that 1 to 2 times a week can be considered minimally sufficient and bathing 3 to 4 times a week might be as good as its going to get… with or without our approval! Older senior adults often develop a habit late in life of relying on an occasional "sponge bath" in between less frequent showers or tub baths.
- When is the best time of day? Things change with different generations and sometimes people revert back to old habits. There was a time when men would often shower in the morning before work whereas the wife and kids had a bath in the evenings before bedtime. Bear in mind their current cognitive status, rituals, and preferences.
- Even the slightest implication that a loved one might "need" a bath infers they are dirty or have an odor, which will surely be met with defiance rather than compliance.
- Provide a nice warm towel straight from the dryer or the microwave.
- Avoid the "B" word altogether. Using terms like "getting cleaned up," "ready to go out," "dressed up," "washed-up," is preferable to the thought of bathing. Words really do matter and the right ones will help avoid any verbal confrontations.

Other astute caregivers, like Martin, have found loving and creative ways to accomplish this task. We're fortunate in that we don't always have to be original in our thinking to find unique and effective solutions, as there are innovative caregivers who willingly share their ideas and experiences. We can follow in their footsteps, explore some of the instances when they have said or done things in a novel way, and then tweak those ideas until they become successful concepts for us. Then we can save the battles for another time or another day

One wife realized that she would have to do something different if she were ever going to get her husband into the shower without yet another argument. So, she invited him to take a shower with her, which he gladly did. Once in the shower together, I understand he put up no resistance to having her help him get washed all over. She said it was a little like when they were newlyweds, but of course, it wasn't quite the same. Now he enjoyed his showers, and she was thrilled to have one less confrontation. It saved time and worry, too. Since he was right there with her, she didn't have to be rushing and fretting about what he was doing while she showered. For her, the sacrifice of solitude and privacy was worth the rewards of peace and tranquility.

A daughter found that letting her mother stay in her gown and robe until much later in the morning gave them both the time to ease into the day. Then, each morning after her mother's shower, then would sit together to enjoy a lovely cup of tea with some cookies, a scone, or a biscuit. On days when the weather was nice, they would have their morning teatime outdoors.

Three mornings a week, one husband would suggest to his wife they should have a special outing that day. He proposed they lunch at one of her favorite places and then go do something fun together. Throughout breakfast, they would talk and make plans to drive around the lake, visit the arboretum, stroll through the local mall to window shop, or visit a nearby pond to feed the fish. As soon as breakfast ended, they cleaned up the kitchen, and then they both got "spruced up" for the events slated for their day out. He offered to let her shower first since she "needed more time to get ready." Both of them enjoyed the excursions, and bathing was no longer an issue.

Caregivers already know that nothing is easy with this disease, and bathing is definitely not the only challenge we face. Activities of daily living are our normal basic routine tasks that people do each day. In healthcare settings these are referred to as "ADL's" which includes bathing, dressing, grooming, eating, toileting, and walking. Throughout our lives, we are used to doing these activities without any assistance from anyone. Irrespective of age, disease, or abilities, we continue to have the desire and determination to do things independently. We don't want any help. Seldom, do we graciously accept offers of assistance, certainly not with our personal care.

Thus, lies the problem when we are trying to be supportive and help provide care for a loved-one. Even when there is no resistance, there's usually some denial of the need for assistance coupled with the "looks," attitudes, and comments. So, how do we ensure these essential activities of daily living are managed appropriately while still treating them at all times as an adult, deserving of respect?

It's important to begin every task with our attention focused on our loved ones. Like it or not, it is almost always going to be about them. And as the disease progresses, caregivers quickly discover it is ALL about them. Our primary objective is to assist them in a manner which allows for some degree of independence - either real or perceived, with the actual completion of a task, such as bathing, dressing, etc., being secondary. With this approach we are more likely to be successful in attaining our desired outcomes. Doing it any other way might get them bathed or dressed; but it will not happen without a huge emotional cost. Most likely it will take twice the time, with everyone ending up frustrated, angry, and stressed.

Implement the concept of being a "care partner" rather than being the caregiver. I doubt that any adult would be enthusiastic about the thought of someone else's taking care of them. One caregiver effectively took this idea to another level. She shared how she consistently reinforces this concept by telling her husband, "We're a team!" and reminds him, "We're in this together!" Approaching everything with this mantra and mindset will certainly start us off in the right direction. With a focus on being care partners, there is a definate shift in the perception of control.

Our loved ones should be allowed to have some degree of active involvement in every task… without exception. It can be as simple as using two wash cloths for bathing—one for them and one for us to actually use. Or having them hold their toothbrush as we apply the toothpaste or asking a father or husband to shake the can of shaving cream as we prepare to help them apply the lather. We never want them to feel like we are taking over a task nor do we want to provide more assistance than they might actually need at that time. There are many steps involved with each of our activities of daily living, but caregivers need to be cautious. We should be mindful of the fact that every single time we do any aspect of a task, regardless of how small or insignificant it might seem, it becomes one less opportunity for them to feel a sense of accomplishment and independence. It should appear as though we are "helping" in much the same way as having their own personal assistant. We want always to make sure they feel as though they are still the one who is in control, even if they're not.

As our loved one's memory diminishes, it becomes increasingly difficult for them to remain self-sufficient with all aspects of their personal care. That, coupled with language skills becoming more impaired, makes it next to impossible for them to carry out our requests for them to handle their ADL's independently. For instance, telling someone to go down the hall and brush his teeth, means he must know the meaning of a lot of words and the names of many objects in order to comply. Additionally, he has to be able to locate and recognize the bathroom and then remember what he was supposed to do upon his arrival. That's a lot of detail to recall for a person with short-term memory problems and attention deficits. It does not mean that they cannot still be independent, but it signals us that we need to observe, supervise, and assist accordingly. In a respectful but subtle way, caregivers might want occasionally to sneak a peek into the shower to see if they are washing or simply getting wet or check their toothbrush for dampness and regular usage. When caregivers assume too much, there are usually going to be some regrets.

As the dementia progresses, people can lose the ability to recognize common everyday items, making simple tasks too complicated. I've seen many people with dementia just staring at a toothbrush or the flatware next to their dinner plate because they don't know what to do next. Adding that pearl of toothpaste or mimicking how you brush your teeth might be just enough of a prompt that would enable them to complete the activity on their own. At meals, resting the fork on the edge of their plate can give them a heads-up about which proper eating utensil to use as well as signal them to eat. By using cues and prompts, you can kick-start the task for them. Then, they can usually continue the activity on their own or with some supervision. If they become distracted, which often happens, you will probably need to start the action once again.

Establishing and maintaining daily routines can make everyone's life easier. These habits are helpful in the early stages and can be a lifesaver as the disease progresses. Performing activities of daily living each day, the same way at the same time, allows our loved ones to have a predictable schedule and creates routines that are easier for them to follow independently, even if only to some small degree. Rote behaviors often enable them to continue to function and complete care tasks somewhat automatically with fewer intentional thoughts for the brain to process.

When caregivers view obstacles and frustrations as problems for which there is a solution, we gain a completely different perspective. This allows us to become proactive caregivers and super sleuths in finding resolutions. Using some creative and pleasurable approaches enables both the caregivers and their loved ones to be more successful. There is never one solution that works for everyone and none will work all the time. Certainly, some answers are going to be easier to find than others, but that's why it's even more critical for us to think outside the box and become innovative in our approaches.

Start with small changes that will make life simple, tasks less complicated, and everything a little more familiar. Here are a few other tips to get you started:
- Encourage them to button blouses or shirts by beginning at the bottom, where the hem on each side can be matched

up, rather than starting at the top where collars can make it confusing to find the first button and correct buttonhole.
- For showers or bathing, use bar soaps rather than liquid body washes.
- Use 2-in-1 shampoo and conditioners and be sure there are no other tubes or containers of other cleaning products in the area.
- Ditch the bra and opt instead for camisoles, sleeping bras or sports bras. These are often more comfortable for many women to wear and easier to put on.
- Enable them to continue to be able to dress independently by replacing buttons and zippers with Velcro® tabs or strips.
- When guys have missed a shave for too many days and are starting to look like a real-life Grizzly Adams, recreate an in-home barbershop setting to get their beards back to a manageable length to ensure a comfortable shave. Sit them down in the kitchen or in the bathroom, cover their shoulders with a towel or cape, use scissors to remove any excessive facial hair that can't stand-up to a razor, apply nice warm cloths to the face, lather up, shave them with a fresh blade in a safety razor and finish off (just like a professional) with a nice little head or shoulder massage, ending with couple of pats of aftershave.
- Consider shoes that are easy to get on, such as slip-ons, loafers, or shoes with Velcro® straps or elastic instead of laces. Find a reason for any shoes without backs, including house slippers or day shoes, to disappear BEFORE your loved one falls...which they will! Ask anyone who works in long-term care, and they will tell you that this style of shoe is just a broken hip waiting to happen.
- Electric toothbrushes can become too difficult to switch on and use independently. As many people with dementia tend to become hypersensitive to noise, families have often found

it best to switch back from electric toothbrushes or electric razors due to either the sound or the vibrations of these items.
- Linger with the body lotion when assisting with grooming and allow loved ones the indulgence of a back, arm, or foot massage. This is one of those pleasurable moments and memories you want to leave with them.

As caregivers, we need to be ever so careful not to take away any opportunities that allow our loved ones to participate, to contribute, to have self-worth. And we can do this by learning and practicing the art of enabling. Again, it not about figuring out how **you** can get something done but accomplishing the task in a way which creates a sense of personal autonomy for a loved one as well as makes each activity of daily living enjoyable and gratifying. This is the true secret to success. It is caring in a way that promotes "wholeness" of a person by reinforcing and preserving their self-esteem and allowing them to "Be all they can be."

> **"When obstacles arise, you change your direction to reach your goal; you do not change your decision to get there."**
> —Zig Ziglar

Reprinted with permission by Ziglar, Inc.

Chapter 18

You Can't Understand What You Don't Know

"My husband doesn't do any of these things! Why are we talking about this!" she said loudly with great exasperation. Quite honestly, we were all a bit shocked at her outburst even knowing that it was her first time to attend a caregiver's support group meeting. For the most part, this meeting had started out much like any of our others. The only exception was that several of the caregivers there that day had been dealing with especially difficult situations. They had immediately jumped right in, detailing concerns that had surfaced since our last meeting. Maybe it was the change of weather, a full moon or something else entirely; but stress levels and frustrations hung heavy in the room that afternoon.

Apparently, this new lady was completely unaware of the many common disease-related behaviors that can accompany a diagnosis of dementia. She certainly made it clear that these discussions were not what she had expected. She then explained to us --mostly to me as the facilitator-- that her husband was very forgetful, he never wandered off, got into things, yelled, or hallucinated. "Furthermore," she said with the tension rising in her voice, "he is a sweet man and does whatever I tell him to do!" There was complete silence in the room.

Suddenly all eyes were on me. So, I said what everyone else was thinking. "Sounds to me like you've been lucky... at least so far."

While it might be possible, I think it would be extremely rare and unusual for a person with Alzheimer's occasionally not to do or say something that would be disruptive to the peace and tranquility in a household. They lack social filters and sometimes act or speak in an inappropriate manner. They get frustrated, lose their tempers, and might even yell or throw something. Unfortunately, some can even become verbally or physically aggressive.

People with dementia have impaired judgment and reasoning and often do things that are unsafe. Safety must be **our** primary concern. Caregivers need to recognize potential hazards and situations that can put our loved ones in harm's way. It's like the old saying about waiting until all the horses have bolted before closing the barn door. You don't want to wait until you have a dangerous kitchen fire or a serious mishap with power tools before you put proper safety precautions into place. We need to stay focused on prevention.

Throughout my life, I have embraced the scouting motto, "Be Prepared." As a former girl scout, den mother, mother of two sons, and now a caregiver, I have learned that it's just plain smart to make plans and be ready for the unforeseen. I like having a Plan A and a Plan B. Sometimes even a Plan C can be wise. Not everybody thinks that way.

Regrettably, if someone is caring for a person with dementia, not having any plans can be a big mistake. Just because something hasn't happened yet, doesn't mean that it might not occur in the future. This is exactly why it is important for all of us to be proactive caregivers and solution seekers. When we are fully prepared physically or emotionally for a potential concern or issue and it doesn't happen, it's much easier to switch gears and re-adjust, than to scramble on the spur-of-the-moment when something startling does occur.

While it is important to hope for the best, we must always be prepared for the worst. And nothing is worse than being caught totally off guard by an unexpected change in behavior, personality, or abilities. By now, you probably have already figured out that every day is a new day, sometimes full of surprises. There are relatively few good surprises with dementia.

I often like to explain dementia in terms of a disease controlled by a dimmer switch. It's not black and white, but shades of colors with occasional fuzzy lines. You or I might be slightly affected by insufficient sleep, seasonal allergies, a headache, or a host of other conditions leaving us feeling less than our best. When a person with any type of dementia is affected by any of these same things, it can make a huge difference in their cognitive abilities or moods that day. It absolutely rocks their boat, often affecting others nearby.

Contrary to the beliefs of many family members, it does matter what is causing our loved one's dementia. It matters greatly. A diagnosis of "dementia" is not enough. Even when we hear "at their age it's probably Alzheimer's" with an insinuation that nothing can be done, we need to know. We would never accept a diagnosis of just "cancer" without being told the type of cancer. Each of the different types or causes of dementia has distinct hallmarks of symptoms. They progress differently and the duration of the specific disease varies. How can we begin to comprehend any of the typical changes or anticipated decline, if we don't first understand the actual cause of their dementia?

I remember when the book ***The 36-Hour Day*** came out in the early eighties and was basically the only book about Alzheimer's and other dementias. At that time, there were only a handful of support groups nationwide, and it was generally believed that there was nothing that could be done for a person with this terrible disease. Everything was different, including our understanding of dementia as well as our approach to care.

Now there are countless books, blogs, and articles available about Alzheimer's, specific dementias, caregiving, and other related topics. Caregivers can attend community educational events, webinars, and conferences. And yet, families continue to be overwhelmed by the daily challenges. There is much to learn and try to understand.

Sometimes it is not merely the present-day challenge or our momentary ineptness that creates these feelings of being overwhelmed but also the uncertainty of tomorrow. There is no way to know what will happen in the next day, the next week, or the next year. Seldom do we ever have a clue as to how many more weeks, months or years are ahead of us.

This is where a support group can be your lifeline. The right support group offers more benefits than most families can even imagine. Throughout the long course of this disease, everything continues to change. Just as no two people with dementia are the same, the needs and desires of caregivers vary every bit as much as the similarities and differences of any individual. And yet, they all benefit from the sense of empowerment that these groups provide.

When someone has never been to a caregiver's support group meeting, the notion of attending can be a bit daunting. The misconception and thought of having to bare your soul and shortcomings in a room filled with strangers is not something that anyone in their right mind would look forward to doing. But the reality is that no one is required to speak or share. Caregivers just need to show up willing to listen and learn. Having a sense of humor can be especially helpful as well as a few tissues. A good support group has laughter, an occasional tear, and a lot of helpful advice from others who are walking the same path. These meetings ensure that no one journeys alone. They are one of the most important resources available to dementia caregivers.

Support groups were never intended to be merely a woe-is-me meeting. Rather, they continue to be a great source for education, referrals, and emotional support. Families can learn about dementia, adopt new coping skills, and acquire effective caregiving techniques. From each other, they receive acceptance, understanding, guidance, and recognition. Equipped with a renewed confidence, they feel stronger in mind and spirit. They are armed with the knowledge needed to tackle the barrage of challenges and be better prepared to expect the unexpected.

Keep in mind that support groups are not all created equal, which is most likely why people tend to either love them or hate them. Sometimes it's because a person has previously attended a poorly conducted or unorganized group resulting in a bad experience. Afterwards that person vows never to return. And, there are some caregivers totally averse to support groups altogether. They have already made up their minds that they don't need "support" and are certain that these groups are simply not for them. But surprisingly, many of these same people have never even attended one meeting. Maybe it's because they didn't know or understand what goes on behind the closed doors. They have never heard the laughter or felt the kindness. They have missed a chance to be reminded that each of us as caregivers is truly doing the best we can, but still want to do better.

One time a woman at a support group meeting shared, with much embarrassment, that she got so mad that morning that she had lost her temper with her husband. "I was actually screaming at him!" she said. Those in the room were completely quiet for only a few seconds, but it seemed much longer before someone else spoke up and said, "…and so?" Those around her were smiling and shaking their heads, with complete empathy and understanding. It is more than probable that if she had told a close friend or family member what she had done, she would have remained full of big-time guilt and remorse.

This story illustrates that sometimes good people do unfavorable things – like yelling. In no way do I mean to imply that screaming at anyone is an acceptable response but merely point out that it can occasionally happen when we are pushed over our stress threshold. The key word to note is "occasionally." If this is happening frequently, you probably need to seek help from a trusted professional, such as a counselor, psychologist, or clergy. For someone that finds themselves losing control on a daily basis (or almost daily), please get help now! This is imperative to your mental health and safety as well as for the person for whom you are caring.

In 1994, President Reagan and his wife Nancy decided to notify the American people of his diagnosis of Alzheimer's disease. In their letter, they were honest and open about his condition hoping it would help to increase awareness of Alzheimer's and create a better understanding of the impact it has on individuals living with this disease as well as their families. At that time, I was working at one of the local chapters of the Alzheimer's Association. Within three months following this very public and heart-wrenching announcement, telephone calls to the Helpline tripled. People began to view this disease differently and without the stigma that had been previously attached. It created both an awareness and acceptance that if this could happen in the White House, it could happen in "my" house.

At that time, President Reagan also noted that he was just one of the millions of people in the United States with the disease. Although in 1998 there were an estimated 2.2 million nationally, it was still generally believed that little could be done to ensure quality of life for a person living with Alzheimer's or address any of the adverse symptoms. People didn't talk openly about the disease nor of the overwhelming responsibility of caring for a loved one with dementia. Caregivers were socially isolated and felt very alone.

Back then there was so little known and even less understood, that families were often embarrassed or at the very least uncomfortable to be around others. Those with dementia were seldom seen out in public. Custodial care was typically provided instead of trying to create an enriching, therapeutic environment, as we do now. They were either cared for privately in their home or placed in nursing homes when a family could no longer cope with the daily emotional and physical demands of caregiving. Those were the only two options.

After Reagan's profound and emotional letter, people started to recognize the importance of seeking information, education, and resources to learn more about this devastating disease. As the numbers of families and caregivers with a longing to learn from others increased, the attendance at Alzheimer's caregivers support groups soared.

Now here we are decades later, with an estimated 5.8 million people living with Alzheimer's in the United States, and families are still seeking out this wonderful opportunity to gain knowledge and support from seasoned caregivers. It continues to be the best place to find a group of positive minded individuals, all with a common desire to learn how to care compassionately and effectively.

If you or someone you know had a terrible experience, then it just wasn't the right group. Perhaps, it was too big, too small, too far or not the best time of day. This is not a disease to go-it-alone. Look for a group that is a good fit for you personally. Consider going back to a previous support group at least one more time or find a different group and try it out a few times. Unless the first time is a complete nightmare, I suggest attending three meetings before making a final decision. There will seldom be all the same people, moods, or issues at that group's meetings, each time.

While I personally believe that meeting in-person with others offers the added benefit of socialization, which is vital to a caregivers' wellbeing, I recognize that for some an online support group might be the best or only option depending on that person's circumstances.

The emotional support we get at these meetings creates the momentum caregivers need to keep going, even when tempted to give-it-up. Much of the time it feels like we are running a marathon, one with no finish line. Nonetheless, we must learn how to pace ourselves, stay ready, keep focused, and be in the moment. We can take a lesson from first-time marathon runners and be inspired by their personal stories. The vast majority of these running the grueling 26 miles of a marathon do so with no aspiration of winning. Yet, most of them train hard almost every day, for months and months, with the strongest determination to succeed. Some hope to beat their personal best time. This race is not always about being the fastest runner. For most, just crossing the finish line is an enormous achievement. As caregivers, we must also remain determined to make all the necessary plans and preparations to keep "running" and complete the race. All the while, we need to strive for our new personal best.

> **"I'm not young enough to know everything."**
> **–Oscar Wilde**

Chapter 19

Monsters After Midnight

Sundays, as I walk through the courtyard after attending mass, the sound of the church bells fills my heart and mind with peace, joy, and cherished memories. Hearing the bells ringing carries me back to a time in my childhood when my cousin Sheri and I would spend Saturday nights at our grandma's house. We lived far apart in different states and saw each other only twice a year, so this was always a special occasion.

The bells were pleasing sounds that woke up both of us girls early on those Sunday mornings, beckoned us out of bed and then serenaded all of us on our walk back home. Grandma lived across the street from the church and she knew everyone, or so it seemed. Both of our parents had been married there, too. So, when we went with Grandma, we never just attended, we made an appearance! Without exception, we arrived much too early, waited until the service was seconds from beginning and then we were marched down the aisle to be seated in the very first pew.

Church bells, anywhere at any time, spark this precious memory, which allows me to recall the delightful details of those mornings and to experience those wonderful emotions all over again. Yesterday after church, I sat quietly for a few minutes in the car just smiling and remembering. Then I thought about how many people take memories for granted as though they will keep them forever and never lose them.

As caregivers, we know and think differently. When we treasure those special people, events, or meaningful times, we hope that we will always be able to remember them. We know how quickly memories can be stolen away. We also understand the importance of memory beyond the blessings of those most valued recollections. Memory has a tremendous impact on all of our emotions, both the good ones and the bad.

When a disease like Alzheimer's or any other related brain disorder affects our brains and memories, it is only natural that emotions will be adversely affected as well. Memory loss takes away information which reassures us, provides comfort and confidence, and enables us to trust.

Memory is what allows us to feel in control of our lives and our thought processes. It enables us to know what is real and what is not. Without memory, many negative emotions and feelings can affect relationships and our sense of well-being. This can also lead to some challenging disease-related behaviors.

All too often a behavior exhibited by someone with cognitive impairment can be misunderstood by families and is viewed purely as a symptom of the disease rather than a natural emotional response. Dementia distorts reality and creates inaccurate perceptions of the world around them. We all have things that push our buttons; but with this disease these emotional buttons might get pushed more easily, seemingly at times with little or no warning.

One morning I could hear Doc yelling at the driver as he got off the bus, and I knew he was angry about something even before he came through the door. He had been coming to the center for over a year and often shared with others how much he enjoyed attending his "memory school." Never had any of us seen him upset --about anything. Ordinarily, he was quiet, polite, and always agreeable. However, that day he was so mad and distraught that he had balled his hands into fists. "That idiot! I'm supposed to be at the hospital right now!" he shouted, "I have an early surgery scheduled!"

Without the slightest hesitation, the first words out of my mouth were an apology with words of regret that no one had been able to reach him. With the utmost sincerity and complete dishonesty, I told him that the surgery had been cancelled at the last minute. "There is no need to worry," I said. Then once more, I expressed remorse and understanding of the difficult situation he had experienced. This was not the time nor place to tell Doc that the paratransit driver was not able to make any additional stops or to remind him that he had been retired for several years. At that moment all he needed to hear were words which would immediately address his emotions, put him at ease, and allow him to regain his normal demeanor. A simple apology, a little empathy, and a tiny lie diffused both his anxiety and frustration.

When we are confronted with difficult situations, it is not the same for us as it is for someone with dementia. The difference is that we have more control over when, what, and how we respond. Dementia is much more than forgetfulness. The disease causes changes in personality, affects control of impulses, and lowers stress thresholds. Memory loss combined with these and other cognitive changes —impaired thinking and reasoning, disorientation, confusion, language difficulties, and shorter attention spans— result in troubling emotional responses and extreme reactions at times. All of which will trigger many of the common behaviors associated with Alzheimer's or other dementias.

As we continue to focus on care with dignity, we need to pay attention to the vast feelings and emotions commonly associated with dementia that make life unpleasant and can be disruptive. This awareness allows us to achieve desirable emotional outcomes as well as provide our loved ones with the best possible quality of life.

Someone living with dementia needs empathy not our sympathy. Because of the disease process, they more readily experience feelings of embarrassment, confusion, anxiety, frustration, paranoia, anger, and/or depression.

Think about times when your children or grandchildren were young and might have displayed any of these emotions. What was happening? How did you comfort them or what did you do to help them feel comfortable, calm, or secure?

Kids often need the help of an adult to be reassured or regain their composure when something troubling occurs. We don't give it much thought; we just do it because we understand their need for our support and guidance to work through it. There was a time that our loved ones, as adults, could overcome any of these feelings and manage just fine on their own, too. But most likely that was <u>before</u> the disease and when they were not dealing with such frequent whirlwinds of emotions.

Let's consider some of the situations that cause our loved ones to experience these same emotions, envision some of the probable resulting behaviors, and design some clear goals for positive outcomes. It will give us a different perspective so when there is a new or disturbing behavior, instead of asking, "Why are they doing that?" or, "What are they thinking?", we might compassionately contemplate "What are they feeling?"

Nighttime can be scary for many people. It's dark outside; there are shadows, and strange sounds. Monsters and the bogeyman can seem real at any age. Little kids often end up crawling in bed with Mommy or Daddy when they get spooked at night or have scary dreams. Many caregivers have shared stories of a loved one getting up at night, roaming the house, checking the doors, or looking out the windows. It's not unusual for blinds or window coverings to be damaged because they are trying to look outside alarmed or distracted by car lights or streetlights trickling in between the slats.

Diane had been one of those nighttime wanderers, which had created huge problems. Even though she and her husband Mack had slept for years in separate beds due to his snoring, the lack of sleep and her increasing anxiety were taking a toll on both of them. She was getting up and down at all hours of the night startled by noises, alarmed by lights outside, and frightened at being alone. At the same time Diane was flipping on lights throughout the house and calling out in search of her mother or father.

This went on for months leaving them both exhausted. Mack tried a variety of suggestions, remedies, and medications prescribed by her physician. Everything was either ineffective or had adverse side effects. Mack was a loving husband and a savvy caregiver, determined to find a solution. I can still picture him calmly sitting there that day at the support group He was beaming with pride and could hardly wait to tell us that he had solved the problem. He got rid of their old beds and bought a queen size bed for them to sleep in together. Now during the night if she got a little restless, he would move closer. She was safe in his arms, loved and protected. This is a fine example of creative caregiving.

Being left alone at home or in the car can also be frightening. Without time awareness, minutes seem like hours. Are they still able to remember where you went and why? What if they think no one is coming back? Often, they panic. I can't tell you how many times, I have personally seen or heard stories of people with dementia wandering the neighborhood, parking lots or stores attempting to find a husband or daughter. Sometimes, just like when a young child is scared or separated from a parent, they just want to go "home" or be with their mother.

All adults want to feel confident and self-assured. It's embarrassing when we forget the name of a dear friend or longtime neighbor. Just about everyone has had these brief memory glitches. When we do, we are reassured by the fact that within a short period of time we are likely to recall that which we have momentarily forgotten. We might feel annoyed or distressed but probably not humiliated. It makes us uncomfortable, but we just move on because we realize that everybody forgets. It's usually not a big deal unless a person has dementia. Then, it can be terribly unsettling.

Even when one knows and understands their diagnosis, a person with memory problems still thinks that there are certain things that they should remember. And, when they don't, they will often talk about being stupid. I am forever reassuring those living with dementia that memory loss makes them forgetful, but it does not affect their intelligence. Often, I remind their family members of that as well. As caregivers, we need to realize that dementia greatly affects our loved one's confidence and self-esteem.

An awareness of disease-related emotional responses can help us, and other family members, better understand how a loved one feels at different times in a variety of situations and respond to their needs accordingly. We know that these feelings are often not rooted in logic but deeply associated with perceptions created by the disease. Unpleasant and disturbing emotions can spark complicated challenges affecting everyone in the house. We need to pay close attention to our loved one's body language and the emotional context of their words, then we can focus our attention directly on achieving pleasant and positive feelings.

Listed below on the far left of each line are some of the common undesirable emotions, which often trigger a disease related behavior. To the right of each one, several of the more desirable feelings are noted which are our aims as caregivers. We need to allow our loved ones to have ownership of the negative emotions regardless of our full understanding. This is not about whether they should or should not feel a particular way. All that matters is how they are feeling and what needs to be done to help them achieve a positive emotional state. We should acknowledge any of those emotions on the left, but then focus our attention on attaining the more pleasant feelings listed next to it on the right.

Confusion – Familiar, clear, understood, certain

Anxiety – Comfortable, relaxed, unworried

Frustration – Untroubled, serene, peaceful
Paranoia – Protected, guarded, trustworthy
Anger – Composed, unruffled, calm, collected
Frightened – Safe, secure, unafraid, brave
Depression – Cheerful, enthusiastic, glad, uplifted

When loving and caring for someone with any type of dementia, the primary goal is always to ensure they have the best possible quality of life. As caregivers, we hope that our actions, words, and deeds will enable them to continue to enjoy life fully every day.

After all, we are the ones that can still remember "Where is Mother?" "When are we going home?" "What am I supposed to do now?" and all the other answers and information to reassure them that they are safe and secure. But it does involve changing our attitudes and expectations in order to provide a more compassionate kind of care. When we can "step into their world," we are able to step back from our reality as needed to be by their side in a troubling place or time. We can be right there with them to make certain they do not feel alone in this frightening world called Alzheimer's.

"Words are also actions, and actions are a kind of words."
–Ralph Waldo Emerson

Chapter 20

If They Can Walk, They Can Wander

Irma caused quite a commotion when she went back "home" to check on her mom. The problem was that her mother, who used to live across the street from her, had died many years ago. You can only imagine her anguish and distress when she discovered a bunch of strangers in her mother's house. She became very belligerent, forcing her way into the house in search of her mom and refusing to accept their preposterous claims that this was their house. When they threatened to call the police, she said, "Good! We'll let them get to the bottom of this!"

All too often caregivers don't realize that for anyone with memory loss, wandering is always a possibility. The reality is that they can, and they will. According to the Alzheimer's Association, six out of every ten people affected by dementia will wander.

Seldom do I have a support group meeting without someone's bringing up the subject of wandering. That begins the great divide. Families tend to think only in terms of they do, or they don't, as though there are only two sides to this critical problem. This is a huge oversight.

Almost daily, we see Silver Alerts on the electronic signs over our highways or read in the news about another missing senior. What most fail to realize is that these individuals are usually not the ones that families have identified as being wandering risks. Caregivers put safeguards in place when they know a loved-one tends to wander. It's most likely to be the ones that "don't" wander that end up lost for endless hours. Too many families have made the mistake of thinking that because their spouse or parent has not wandered, they never will. Constantly, I remind families, "If they can walk, they can wander."

In the minds of many, wandering problems associated with dementia bring images of only those that become lost after walking away from home or while driving. There is just not enough awareness about how easily and frequently this occurs. People with memory problems find themselves in situations in which they become confused, disorientated, and unable to find their way. Moreover, it happens both innocently as well as unintentionally. People with Alzheimer's or other dementias wander away and get lost for a variety of reasons…in all kinds of places. They get lost in shopping malls, airports, large retail stores, and special events locations.

Frequently they get lost while traveling on vacation. Families have recalled countless stories of their loved ones getting lost when they were together on a trip, hundreds of miles away from home. Always with extreme anguish, they begin the retelling, still in disbelief of how quickly it all happened.

At a huge luxury resort in Mexico, a man woke up from his nap and thought his wife had gone to dinner without him, so he left the room, thinking he would meet her at the restaurant. At the time, she was taking a shower and never heard him leave. His family and the security guards frantically searched for hours before finding him.

Thinking his father was "not that bad," one son decided to take his dad out of state to see one of the big annual Bowl games. The trip there was tiring but uneventful. Before the game started, they both stopped by the men's room. The son waited for his father right outside of the restroom door where they had entered but never saw his father come out. Unbeknownst to the son, there were two exits. That, combined with the massive crowds, created an exceedingly stressful situation for both the father and the son. Despite the best efforts of several of the stadium security and staff, they didn't find his dad until after the game ended, when almost everyone had left the stands.

I've heard hundreds of stories about people with dementia becoming lost in other crowded places, too. Wives and mothers have gotten lost at the Vatican, the symphony, and Walmart. Husbands and fathers have disappeared on the way back to the parking lot following a grandchild's soccer game, in Home Depot, and during a routine stroll around the block. One man, vacationing with his family on a cruise ship, was missing so long that the Captain was within minutes of declaring a "Man Overboard" alert.

Even in familiar places, our loved ones can become disoriented, and get lost. Marvin was always careful and seldom let his wife, Maxine, out of his sight. As her Alzheimer's worsened, their routines grew more sacred. They got into the habit of eating at the same neighborhood restaurant for an early dinner, five nights a week. Saturdays were sandwiches or pizza at home. Then, on Sundays, they went to their daughter's house. It was a good set schedule that allowed Marvin to provide worry-free meals which he didn't have to cook. It worked out nicely for both of them. As regular diners, the restaurant was comfortable and familiar; all the staff knew them and understood about Maxine's disease. That's what made the incident so inconceivable.

One day as Marvin was visiting with their regular waitress, Maxine got up as usual, and went by herself to the Ladies' room. Only, this time she didn't come back. After several hours of searching, someone spotted her, hiding in a car, in another parking lot that was quite a distance from the restaurant.

Since Maxine's language skills were impaired, no one will ever know for sure the exact details of what happened that day. Based on bits and pieces of information, Marvin surmised that she turned the wrong way when leaving the restroom and went out through the kitchen instead of returning to the dining room. Since it was during a delivery, the staff was busy, and the back doors were wide open.

Maxine said that she decided to get into the car (which she mistakenly thought was their car), because some strange people (who kept shouting her name) were after her. These strangers were, of course, the people trying to help locate her.

Her perception of being in harm's way is one of the reasons that many people with dementia can be especially difficult to locate. They hide or seek shelter for a variety of reasons; they get frightened and panic, seek protection from extreme weather conditions, or just need a place to rest. Therefore, people with dementia are often found in storm drains, under piles of leaves, in a stranger's unlocked car, behind a neighbor's shrubs, or in the shade of someone's backyard. The list could go on and on but the point is, they are often not out in the open.

Too often, caregivers run into a store for a couple of items and leave their loved-one alone in the car for "just a few minutes." Since that person has short-term memory loss; they are not able to recall the reassuring comments from their family about, "Wait here, I'll be right back." Minutes soon begin to seem like hours. The next thing you know, they get anxious, start to panic, leave the car, and go in search of their daughter, son, or spouse. If everyone is lucky, someone will see them wandering around the parking lot or in the store. I always hope that they either have some identification with them or are capable of correctly stating their full name and address. Otherwise, those few minutes really can turn into hours of a search and rescue attempt for that same family, who was in such a hurry.

Keep car keys out of sight. Even when a person with dementia who has not driven a car for years, they can forget that, too. In the brief time that a caregiver turns to put away grocery items or goes to use the toilet, keys have been snatched for a variety of quick errands, that suddenly come to mind upon seeing the keys lying around somewhere out in the open. It seems to prompt them to do something that they might have done routinely in the past. In their mind, they might be going to pick up milk at the local supermarket, fill the car with gas or for a follow-up doctor's appointment. These are only a very few of the examples which families have shared with me. Sometimes even when the drive there was managed without an incident, the real problem arose when they couldn't remember where they had parked the car. It wasn't even a matter of remembering which row, but rather which parking lot.

One man stole an employee's keys off the kitchen counter in a rural nursing home located about forty miles from San Antonio. He had lived there for many years and seemed content. In all that time, he never once talked about leaving or tried to wander away. The staff immediately notified his family, the sheriff's office, and highway patrol.

Fortunately, one of his sons found him at a South San Antonio neighborhood tavern his father had frequented more than a decade before. He was casually sitting at the bar, drinking a beer. The timeline indicated that this man must have driven straight from the nursing home to that tavern. When the son told him how worried everyone had been and asked him why he drove there, his dad replied matter-of-factly, "I was thirsty."

The subject of wandering is one of my most serious soapbox crusades. In actuality, I could fill a book with true stories on the perils of wandering. It grieves me to remember the many times that these tales did not have happy endings. I hope that something I have said in this chapter might help save even one life, one person from suffering serious injuries, or one family from the gut-wrenching agony when a loved-one is missing.

Should your loved-one disappear from anywhere at any time, act fast. If you're not able to locate them within ten to fifteen minutes at the very least, call 91, and get assist with the search. Be very clear to whomever you contact that your loved-one has severe memory loss and may not respond appropriately. Everyone needs to understand that time is critical.

Also, do not assume that local authorities will arrange for search and rescue dogs to assist with a search. In many communities, this request and/or contact must come from the family. Most importantly, you should know that when a person with dementia is not located within twenty-four hours, more than half of them are found with injuries, in serious condition, or dead.

The first time an incident occurs is certainly going to be the most frightening and exasperating. It catches families totally off guard because "they never did this before." If we are not actively listening to their words and emotions, we can miss some of the warning signs. Then, seemingly out-of-the-blue, they might decide, like Irma, to go visit a family member. Sometimes they are reliving the past and might suddenly leave to go to "pick up the kids" or to go to work. Holidays, large family gatherings, or crowds of strangers, will often cause a person with dementia to literally escape to a more peaceful or familiar place.

Notify all your nearby neighbors for both their alertness as well as their understanding. Having a family member with memory problems or any form of dementia should not be embarrassing, nor should it be a secret. It is in everyone's best interest and your loved one's wellbeing that others know.

A skilled nursing and rehab facility contacted the daughter of a 92-year-old woman with Alzheimer's, to notify her that she would need to find another place for her mother. The facility staff felt that they could no longer ensure her safety. It seems that her mom was frequently going out the side exit doors, rolling down the ramp in her wheelchair, and going "home." Although she was unable to walk, she was clearly able to wander away from that facility.

Unfortunately, the vast majority of families often wait until something happens before putting safeguards in place. I cannot stress enough the danger involved. There are countless stories of those that wandered and did not survive. In writing this chapter, I shared with my husband the story of the woman with Alzheimer's who got lost at the Dallas Fort Worth International airport some years back. Since I couldn't recall exactly when it happened, I decided to search online for more information. Even I was shocked to see over six stories – just on the first screen – of women with dementia missing from airports throughout the country.

We may never know why many of these events happen. However, some measures might have prevented many of them or facilitated a safe return. Be both cautious and proactive. Take preventative measures to avoid problems before they occur. Maybe you will be one of those lucky families that never have to deal with wandering issues. A myriad of families will tell you that it is far better conscientiously to plan for the possibility, rather than procrastinate and respond afterwards.

From my soapbox, one last time, I will tell you again. If they can walk, they can wander. It happens too often, too quickly, and in too many families. It is not worth taking the risk.

"It wasn't raining when Noah commenced the Ark."

Chapter 21

How About a Drink?

You might say that my mother became a problem drinker late in life. Of course, not the kind of drinking problem that usually comes to mind when we hear those words. Her problem was the same one that is all too common with seniors. She didn't drink enough fluids to stay properly hydrated.

As my mother's physical health declined, she became less active and had little interest in drinking or eating. Just like so many older adults who don't drink enough liquids, dehydration was a frequent issue. In this day and time, it seems as if everyone in the entire world —except for our loved ones— recognizes the benefits of drinking water. For many seniors, there lies one of the problems. It's often more than just understanding the importance of fluid intake. The constant pestering from families in hopes of persuading them to drink more water often becomes just a battle of the wills. It easily becomes more of a control issue and less of a hydration concern. Neither side wins, and everyone feels frustrated.

Another one of the problems is that some people, especially many seniors such as my mother, just don't like to drink water. One time when the subject of drinking at least 64 ounces per day came up in a casual conversation with some friends, my mother boldly declared that she drank almost that much every day. I seriously thought she was just kidding or being sarcastic. Later when I questioned her about her comment, she said with an elfish grin, "How do you think I make my pot of coffee?"

With my mom, I knew that her daily coffee was important to her and decided to follow the first Caregiver's Rule, "Pick your battles." (If this rule is not already carved in stone, it should be!) At that time, I decided to consider her coffee as a good-enough, second-best drink since water would never even be on her short list. I had already figured out that any beverage she was willing to drink was certainly going to be better than having nothing at all. I would keep in mind that a fluid is a fluid and be thankful she was at least drinking something.

Most days before my mother's health diminished, her morning was filled with cups of coffee, and a few glasses of Sprite® got her through her afternoons. During her last few months, she got down to only one partial cup of coffee in the morning and would sip the same single glass of soft drink for the remainder of the day. That's when I knew we were heading down a dangerous path.

In this book, I talk a lot about the mistakes I made with my dad. I can honestly say that when my mother started having critical issues with dehydration, I was smart enough to know that if Mother had not liked water and hardly drank it for almost eighty years, she certainly wasn't going to partake of it now. I fully understood and accepted that regardless of what I did or said, I was never going to get her to drink water. Therefore, I needed a serious take-action plan which would focus on other liquids.

My first weapons of choice for my mom in this crusade against dehydration were fruit-flavored gelatin cups and popsicles. Keeping an adequate supply of both on hand and offering them frequently throughout the day was helpful. In addition, making slight adjustments to her meals provided some additional sources of fluids from foods with high water content.

There is no question that drinking water is good for all of us and provides a key element of a healthy lifestyle. Adequate water consumption enables the body to flush out the toxins and keeps our systems in balance. But when we can't get them to drink water, we need to find other good options that will be appealing to them.

Serious problems occur when dehydration is not promptly recognized and treated. It is one of the most frequent causes of emergency room visits and hospitalizations for those 65 years of age and older. Inadequate levels of fluids often result in constipation or urinary tract infections. Dehydration can also cause a sudden change in blood pressure upon standing, which often causes falls. Sometimes, it results in serious consequences.

A quick and easy test that you can do at home is the same as the one generally used by health professionals. Gently pinch the skin on the forearm, to assess for loss of normal skin elasticity. When the body is in a dehydrated state, the skin is slow to return to the normal position. Other indications are headaches, persistent fatigue, dark circles under the eyes, or decrease in urine output.

Below are some of the specific foods and ideas which will assist in promoting good health and maintaining proper levels of hydration. As you read these suggestions of ways to avoid dehydration, remember that all other medical problems and existing health factors need to be considered especially if someone is already on a therapeutic diet. In those instances, you should always talk first to your physician or a registered dietitian before making any modifications.

- Offer and encourage water and/or juice at scheduled times throughout the day – six to ten times – depending on "successful" amounts.
    - o Try offering lesser amounts more frequently throughout the day. Offering six ounces in a small juice glass will be less overwhelming than an iced tea size glass filled to the top.
    - o Observe the person's preferred temperature for beverages, keeping in mind that people might prefer room temperature (like tap water), cold with no ice, or with a lot of ice.

- Adjust menus and meal plans to include more fresh fruits and vegetables which have a higher water content. These would include strawberries, grapefruit, cucumbers, spinach, and iceberg lettuce. Even cooked, both asparagus and broccoli have a high-water content.
- Serve a cup of soup, salad, or a small glass of either fruit juice or vegetable juice <u>before</u> both lunch and dinner meals. When that is the only thing in front of them, they are more likely to eat or drink it.
- When planning meals, include foods that are made with water or milk, such as puddings, flavored gelatin or soups. Consider making hot cereals, like oatmeal, with extra milk and top with fresh fruit for breakfast.
- Try encouraging milk with the evening meal. Think of milk as a bonus beverage. It is not only a healthy fluid but drinking milk at supper or with a bedtime snack can also enhances nighttime sleeping. It is rich in tryptophan, which produces sleep inducing brain chemicals.
- Offer healthy snacks between meals such as raw celery sticks, cherry tomatoes, or melon balls. Raw baby carrots are great, too, and have more water content that full sized carrots.
- Remember other favorite or special treats which can be offered throughout the daytime or evening hours for snacks
    - Popsicles, frozen fruit bars, sherbet, or ice cream
    - Root beer floats or sherbet with lemon-lime carbonated beverages
    - Chocolate or strawberry flavored milk
    - Milkshakes or smoothies made with fresh strawberries, peaches, or blueberries
    - Yogurt cups or frozen yogurt
    - Individually packaged applesauce or fruit cups packed in juice

While I have found several other sources that agree with my mom in the water versus coffee debate, I still personally believe that drinking water is one of the healthiest things we can do for our bodies and to maintain good health. I am thankful that there have finally been studies that recognize that fluids are fluids when it comes to hydration. As caregivers, we have enough problems on our hands without being encouraged by the healthcare community to mess with their daily morning cups of coffee or mealtime glasses of favorite soft drinks.

In 2014, a study done in the United Kingdom found no difference in the hydration status between those drinking coffee versus those who drank the same amounts of water. If my mother were still here, she would have loved to say, "I told you so."

Those with Alzheimer's or other dementias typically have a reduced sense of thirst or lose all recognition of the body's need to drink so they don't get thirsty at all. Some people are convinced that they already consume plenty of fluids each day. Many older adults, with or without cognitive impairment, self-restrict their fluid consumption to avoid having an embarrassing accident. Then there are others, like my mom, that clearly do not drink water at all.

For all these reasons, caregivers need to be both creative and persuasive. Not bossy. We cannot make them drink, but we can encourage and hope for the best. They might promise you that they will start doing better tomorrow. But that's probably not going to happen. So, it might be wiser to let them drink whatever they are willing to drink and modify their meals and snacks to enable them to enjoy "eating" their water. With fingers crossed, maybe the drinking problem will be resolved.

> **"You cannot push anyone up a ladder unless he be willing to climb a little himself."**
> **— Andrew Carnegie**

Chapter 22

The Power of Praise and Compliments

We had just completed all of the enrollment paperwork for Frank, Kathy's father, to start coming to the day center a few times a week. Although she thought her dad would enjoy being there, her main concern was giving her mother a break from the daily demands of caring for someone with dementia. She voiced the same concern that I have heard hundreds of times before. She felt as if she was already losing one parent to this disease and didn't want to lose the other. Her mother was determined to care for her husband at home but was becoming increasingly frail and experiencing some health issues directly related to the stress of being a full-time caregiver.

Suddenly Kathy seemed slightly subdued, saying she had one last question, "Is there a dress code?" Since the members attending the center pretty much wore whatever they wanted to wear, I was not exactly sure how to answer. Because it was summer, some wore shorts and tennis shoes. Other men, regardless of the season, wore jeans, khakis, or casual slacks year-round. There were a couple of retired professionals, who usually wore sport coats just as though they were still going to the office.

There wasn't any formal dress code or policy. So, I explained that basically everyone tended to dress according to his or her own personal style and level of comfort. Then added in a lighthearted tone, "But, no one is allowed to wear pajamas."

I asked Kathy why she seemed so concerned. She explained that shortly after her father retired, he started occasionally wearing jumpsuits. Then, he began wearing them often. Now he wore them every day and everywhere. It had become quite an issue with his wife and family because he had refused to go anywhere if he couldn't go in his treasured jumpsuits. In addition, Frank no longer believed it was necessary to change his personal dress code when attending church on Sundays or when going to funerals. "After, all," he told his wife and daughter, "do you really think that God cares what I wear?" Well, we certainly didn't care.

From then on, Frank showed up every day wearing a big smile and his favorite jumpsuit. He was a lot of fun, very sociable and always lending a hand to help staff or other members. When Frank was at the center, he loved telling the ladies how pretty they looked and could be quite captivating. The ladies in return oozed compliments right back at him.

One morning, a few months later, Frank showed up in slacks and a collared shirt. We were all taken by surprise. Something was surely up. As he came in the door, I greeted him saying he looked especially handsome and must have a very important meeting that morning. We figured that maybe he had a doctor's appointment or something significant, even though he never would have dressed differently before. Kathy was just standing there looking as puzzled as we were.

"Nope!" he said, "I just got mighty tired of looking like a bum." Ah… the power of praise and compliments. It was the first time I realized that dignity is actually visible.

Praise is the perfect example of how a little thing can make a big difference. Angie's daughter Diane was amazed at the change in her mother's attitude since her previous visit a few months before. Angie lived full time with her married daughter Doris. Every few months her other daughter Diane would come from out of state to spend some time with her mother as well as give her sister a respite.

Diane said that during these visits she would get up a little earlier than her normal time to have a peaceful cup of coffee before attempting to get her mom up. She spoke of how she dreaded this morning ordeal filled with arguments and aggravation that occurred every time she tried to get Angie out of bed and dressed. With a hint of both pleasure and surprise in her voice, she shared that this morning had been different.

By the time Diane heard her mother stirring around and went into her bedroom, she found Angie fully dressed and making the bed. The only thing she needed from her daughter was help with deciding which earrings she should wear that day.

Since Diane's last visit, Angie had been attending the day center. She had always loved playing poker and now looked forward to the daily blackjack games, where she was often the only woman playing. Her memory might have faded but as soon as she sat down at the table with poker chips in front of her, she became a serious card shark. There's no doubt about the pleasure she derived from beating the guys at "their" game. Most of all, I think she enjoyed the attention of all the "handsome" men there. The men appreciated Angie's jokes and humor, pulled out her chair in the dining room, and told her what a "good-looking woman" she was.

As a single mother, Angie had reared both of her daughters all on her own. For most of her life she was accustomed to being in a man's world, and now when she was at the center, she was back in her element. She had things to do, a place to go and men to charm.

When someone we love has dementia, caregivers might have to work a bit harder to help him or her continue to feel appreciated as a parent, spouse, or friend. Praise and compliments meet our basic psychological needs for affection and attachment. Caregivers use these accolades to acknowledge and show with our words that our loved ones are still valuable. It is not a secret, to us or to our loved one, that people with dementia do change. But praise has the power to reassure loved ones that we continue to love and respect them — just the way they are. It is such a simple and necessary way to ensure that their sense of self-worth doesn't disappear along with their memory.

It's understandable how a family member caring for a parent or spouse can overlook the importance of these small but powerful comments. As caregivers, we tend to get so caught up in everything that is going on around us that we sometimes take these things for granted. It only takes a moment to praise another. Praise is to people like sunshine is to flowers; it is necessary to flourish.

Compliment loved ones on their good-looking outfit, great smile, beautiful blue eyes, or positive attitude. Acknowledge their good sense of humor saying, "You always make me laugh," or recognize they are a good person with a "warm and caring heart." Caregivers express genuine praise when we congratulate our loved ones for being talented, smart, kind, helpful, interesting, trustworthy, or polite. Short, simple, thoughtful words of kindness.

My dad was always concerned about his appearance and prided himself on looking nice. Before his retirement, he wore a suit and necktie every day to work. Growing up in St. Louis in the thirties, he recalled a time when only poor and needy kids wore jeans or tennis shoes. So, he was never comfortable dressing that causal and wore those items only out of necessity for working in the yard, around the house, or on a fishing trip. For as long as I can recall, even in his last years when he was living in a memory care community, Dad preferred collared shirts, slacks, and leather loafers. Thinking back on all the years he went to community senior centers for weekly pinochle games and activities, I sometimes wonder what gave him the greatest satisfaction. Although I know how much he always enjoyed playing cards, I am also aware of the immense pride and pleasure he derived from compliments on his dress and appearance from his peers. It made his day whenever anyone told him that he looked handsome or was a snappy dresser, even when the compliment came from his daughter!

One of the best examples of an astute caregiver and the potential for praise is a story about socks. Iris laid out Art's clothes for the day just as she had done for her husband every morning for the last year. This had enabled him to remain somewhat independent and able to continue to dress himself with limited supervision. She left the room for only a short while to check on something only to remember that she forgot to lay out his socks. By the time she returned Arthur had not only found his socks in the drawer but had managed to put them on...all eight pairs. Iris said that despite this unforeseen outcome, she was sincerely impressed. So, she sat down on the bed next to her husband and proudly complimented him for taking the initiative and putting on all of these socks, on his own. Iris lavished him with praise as he respectfully removed each pair with her by his side. "Good job, Art," she said, "this pair matches." "And this pair is a nice match, too." "Look here, Honey, another good match!" The encouraging dialogue and compliments continued until he got down to one last final pair. Because Iris chose to show adoration over annoyance, it was a pleasant and successful day for both of them.

Be it a gentle touch of acknowledgement, a wink of approval, or a smile of admiration, even the smallest gesture has the power to make a big difference...to any of us.

"A compliment is something like a kiss through a veil."
— **Victor Hugo**

Chapter 23

Grateful Hearts and Happy Souls

Begin the day with a thankful heart. It sounds trite and almost impossible if you are caring for a loved-one with dementia. We see this saying on signs, refrigerator magnets and almost everywhere these days. Gratitude is a crucial key to keeping a caregiver's life in balance. In fact, numerous studies have shown a direct link between gratitude and wellness. It can change our attitudes, and expectations, as well as our perspective. As caregivers, practicing gratitude positively affects our well-being as well as those for whom we care.

Gratitude allows us to be happier, healthier caregivers. Living with constant stress, coping with daily challenges, and watching loved ones slowly decline take a toll on the physical and emotional health of dementia family caregivers. An attitude of gratitude has proven to increase happiness, decrease depression, and foster resilience. Expressing our feelings of gratefulness induces the relaxation response thus reducing stress and promoting better sleep.

A sign hangs in my home that says, "There is Always, Always, Always, Something to Be Thankful For." Although when a caregiver is overwhelmed by all the endless tasks and emotions of caregiving, it can be hard to recall this simple saying, let alone put it into practice. Once gratitude becomes part of your daily life, it's easier to find reasons for which to be thankful.

You might be grateful that you still have your health or woke up with an abundance of patience. Perhaps, you both laughed together during breakfast, he winked at you or she smiled and said, "I love you." Or being grateful that at least one of you still has a sense of humor by the end of the day, even during those moments when neither of you can agree on what is truly funny.

We might be thankful for family, friends or neighbors who are willing to help and support us from one day to the next. It's wise to graciously accept their offers of time and talents without hesitation. My experience has been that most caregivers are far better at giving than receiving. There are times when, as caregivers, we are too overwhelmed to know how to respond to a friendly solicitation. And those desiring to help us will often need some direction as to what would be useful for us.

Throughout this journey our needs and stamina will be ever changing, as is everything else. When family and friends inquire, consider these suggestions:

- Use post-it notes on a bulletin board or refrigerator to indicate specific tasks or errands that would be beneficial.
- Jot down items in a notebook as they come to mind for others to select, according to their personal preference and available time. For someone that enjoys cooking, a homemade dinner casserole can be easy to prepare and deeply appreciated.
- If nothing comes to mind, ask them if you can call them at a future date. Have them write down their name, number and offer in a book or on a list to which you can refer when that need arises. Then call on them at that time.
- Remember that others offer because they **want** to help. Allow them the gratification of giving you this gift of love and friendship, a genuine gesture of care and concern.

My father was always good about expressing his appreciation to others. For quite a few years, almost every Wednesday was date night with my dad. It was much like a double date since most of the time it included my husband and Dad's girlfriend. Being over ninety years of age, he loved telling anyone that would listen that he had a girlfriend. Always adding that he was crazy about her. However, that's another story for another time.

So, every week, without exception, there was the same rehearsed, unscripted conversation in the car. He thanked us for taking them out to dinner. In response, we would thank him for going with us. He would tell us how much he enjoyed our company, and we say that we loved spending time with them. As we merged into the busy Dallas traffic, he would tell us that he sure was glad that he didn't drive anymore. We would quickly add that we were really, really glad he didn't drive either! We all laughed and by the time we had arrived back home, all of our hearts were full of the love of family and gratitude for the opportunity to spend another evening together. It can be just that simple.

Imagine starting each day hearing words of gratitude from another person. As caregivers, we have that power to give our loved ones that gift. Every expression of appreciation becomes yet another loving act of kindness. On a daily basis, we can voice our appreciation for their help, thoughts, or opinions. We can thank them just for taking the time to listen, smile, or for a multitude of other reasons.

Probably like many of you, when our children were young, we seldom missed an opportunity to say please and thank you. We wanted them to hear those words often each day because it was an important part of teaching them good manners and respectful behavior towards other people. In my family, we referred to "please" and "thank you" as magic words. Now as caregivers, we can use these same words to demonstrate our respect and gratitude for our loved ones. As an adult I discovered that they still are magical and powerful for improving relationships with anyone, under any circumstances.

I've had family members tell me that their loved one knows how they feel, but that's not enough. It's especially important now, with this disease, that we express our gratitude with words. I would often tell my dad that he had always been a wonderful father. And now I was glad that I could help him and do things for him. Tell your mother that you're glad that you can be there for her. Let her hear your words. Remind your spouse that you enjoy being with him or her, that you are proud to be their husband or wife. Saying, "You are such a gentleman," is a terrific way to thank husbands and fathers for opening a door or pulling out a chair. "You make me happy," is a pleasing comment to anyone's ears.

Express the same appreciation for their offers to help as you do when they are actually assisting in some way. There are times when we are just not able to accept their offer of assistance for one reason or another. The task might be beyond their ability, surpass time constraints, or exceed our limitations of patience at that moment. Taking a few minutes to convey our appreciation for their desire to help is going to be more meaningful and uplifting than just saying, "No, thank you." When we respond gratefully, we can respectfully acknowledge their thoughtfulness rather than just declining their offer.

Show gratitude for any efforts, regardless of outcomes. The only thing worse than seeing a loved one fail at something is the day comes when he or she just gives up and stops trying to do anything at all. At the end of the day, we want them to feel like they are good, not "good-for-nothing." Frequent acknowledgement and words of thankfulness can help prevent that from occurring sooner as the result of a total loss of self-confidence, rather than later due to limitations brought on by the progression of the disease.

"Well done," "Very nice," and "I appreciate you" can be very inspiring words that will sincerely boost their ego. The list of words to express gratitude and appreciation is practically endless. Recognize any and all of their personal accomplishments, whether big or small. We can seldom thank a person too much or acknowledge their accomplishments too often. All these small gestures of kindness will come right back to us, too. What makes them feel good, makes us feel even better.

When we practice gratitude, we can fully enjoy being "in the moment" with our loved ones with an increased awareness of personality traits or capabilities remaining, despite this terrible disease. Rather than becoming emotionally entangled by the sadness of all the things they can no longer do, we can thankfully acknowledge their existing strengths and abilities. Again, we can find something for which to be thankful.

As odd as it might sound, as my dad's disease progressed, many of my previous frustrations became some of the reasons for which I was most grateful. When he started repeating a story or asking the same question three times in a row, I was grateful that he still wanted to talk and share, and that he could. When he was trying to tell me something and too many words were missing, I was grateful for the remaining words. When he started to walk away without his walker, I was grateful that he could still walk.

And during those heartbreaking times when he was so unsure of who I was, I embraced the memory and remained happy and grateful that my entire life, he had lovingly referred to me as his "favorite daughter." Even though I knew, that as his only child, there was never any competition.

> **"Gratitude is not only the greatest of all virtues, but the parent of all others."**
> — Marcus Tullius Cicero

Chapter 24

When We Know Better

For most of my life I've been smart enough to know that I'm simply not smart enough. This little fact has served me well through the years and allowed me to be successful in almost all my endeavors. There are times in our lives when we realize that we don't need to know all about everything. We only need to know enough at that given moment. As caregivers, we have to realize critical gaps in our knowledge can be filled by listening and learning from others, who do in fact know more than we do.

Caring for a loved one with a progressive neurological disease, such as Alzheimer's, is truly one of those times when we realize we must know more than we know today. We are living and caring for others at a time when there is a tremendous amount of Alzheimer's and dementia research being conducted throughout the world. And with the internet, it's become easy to stay abreast of the latest discoveries and revised best practices for dementia care. We need continually to seek this updated information and deepen our understanding for us to be more competent, compassionate, and capable. Regardless of how good most of us might be already, we still want to "do better."

It wasn't until after several years of caring for my dad that I was able to understand why caregivers have such difficulty responding appropriately to the changing needs of their loved ones. Before then I would often wonder why caregivers would sometimes say or do things which made no sense at all. It reminds me of the time when we watch a scary movie. We are practically holding our breaths as the tension begins to mount. The music dramatically changes as the suspense surges and our hearts race. Then, when the actress reaches for the doorknob, we are all thinking, possibly yelling, "Don't Open the Door!" As a spectator in the comfort of the real world, we know it's not a good idea. What is she thinking? Why is she doing that? These are some of the same questions which others might ask about any of us, family caregivers. What are we thinking and why are we doing this or that? Sometimes the honest answer simply is we are not thinking. Certainly, we are not thinking clearly or logically.

Years ago, I probably could have picked up almost any book about dementia care and would have accepted all the information at face value. Often with many of the books I have read in more recent years, written by experienced healthcare professionals, I now find myself thinking that undoubtedly this author has never been the primary caregiver for a loved-one with Alzheimer's. While the information stated is academically correct and offers great advice for dementia care in a community healthcare setting, it is seldom practical or realistic for a family caring for a loved one at home. In theory the advice sounds good but for a seasoned caregiver it is almost laughable.

Caregivers soon recognize that the best source for hands-on guidance, tips and techniques comes not from any one person but rather a variety of experienced people – healthcare professionals, paid caregivers, and especially from a lot of other family caregivers. From others we can learn to adjust our expectations, adapt the environment to accommodate their changing strengths, abilities, and limitations; as well as modify both our attitudes and approaches.

It's no secret that what works for one, might not work for another. What works today, may or may not work tomorrow. As caregivers, we need an all-you-can-learn-buffet of ideas and suggestions. Then, we can pick and choose what we think will work best for us and our personal situation at that particular time. At the very least, these options help us find a starting point for the changes and improvements needed for us to become the quintessential caregiver to which we aspire. It's a learning experience that plants seeds of knowledge in our minds and our hearts. As it strengthens us both intellectually as well as emotionally, we become savvy caregivers.

When we know better, we learn to look for other reasons for **abrupt** changes in memory, behaviors, or gait. The definitive word is "abrupt". It's important for caregivers to understand that with Alzheimer's, noticeable changes do not occur overnight. This is a disease that progresses slowly, with subtle deviations in cognitive functioning or physical performance. Experienced caregivers do not just assume that the dementia is merely progressing, but rather look for other possible causes for these unexpected changes.

It would be great if caregivers could magically become Sherlock Holmes when dealing with any disease related behaviors. So often throughout the course of this disease, we could benefit from his astute powers of observation and deduction. Those skills would allow us to discover the roots of many problems and the triggers for most behaviors.

Our loved one's body language needs to be carefully observed and monitored since illness, pain, or discomfort are often communicated through new or worsening behaviors. Sudden inconsistencies from their recent norms are considered early warning signs of another possible health related concern. Increased agitation, restlessness, cursing, or combativeness can be the result of an undiagnosed physical or medical problem rather than a cognitive issue.

It's important for us to recognize that people with dementia still have all the same health problems that everyone else experiences, but they are often unable to tell us with their words. Just like us, they get headaches, have diarrhea or constipation, arthritis, colds, allergies, upset stomachs, and many other ailments. Sometimes it is difficult for them to even understand what is going amiss with their body: there is only an awareness of pain or discomfort. Their ability to describe symptoms, details or location is severely limited. Thus, experts estimate about 50% of older adults with dementia are under-treated for pain.

When my dad broke his back, he complained only of stomach pains. We had no idea he had fallen, or anything was wrong with his back. When his caregiver called me early on a Monday morning, he said my father refused to get up because his stomach was hurting, and he wanted to go back to sleep. By the time I got there twenty minutes later, it was a slightly different story. He was glad to see me; said he was fine. As soon as I began to help him get out of bed, his "stomach" pains returned.

My first thought was constipation or maybe an impaction. When you work in this profession long enough, you realize how tricky it is properly to monitor bowel movements when people self-toilet. Then throw in memory problems, and you quickly discover that you can't rely on them to give you any information regarding their stools or frequency. Although this is not a pleasant topic, it is necessary for caregivers to have a crucial awareness of this condition, since people with dementia can in fact die from severe complications caused by fecal impactions.

All I knew for certain that morning was that my dad almost never complained and rarely had so much as a headache, body ache or pain. If he said he hurt, then I knew absolutely that something was wrong. By that Wednesday, he had been examined twice by his physician and following the results of some lab tests, her professional diagnosis was, "I don't know." We encountered almost the same outcome at the emergency room. Of course, a tad in their defense, while at each of these places, Dad was very calm, friendly, mannerly, and charming as though we were there for a social visit. He voiced no complaints to the medical staff; but when asked directly, he would confirm that his stomach did "hurt a little." He only seemed to wince and groan when he was getting out of bed, the car, or off the exam table, sometimes reaching back in the area of his kidneys. It was only after much persuasion that the physicians decided to focus additional tests and attention on something other than his stomach or urinary tract. They determined that two of the vertebrae in his lower back were fractured. His stomach was fine.

Another mystery can be solved by considering that a urinary tract infection (UTI) might be the cause of sudden changes. As people age, they become more susceptible to UTI's for a variety of reasons. For people with dementia, early indicators of a UTI are often detected by abrupt deviations in their functioning or behavior, long before they become traditionally symptomatic. Almost overnight, we will notice increased confusion, changes in their gait, or observe them leaning while walking or sitting. That's when it's time promptly to seek medical attention instead of waiting for the other usual symptoms to develop and the infection to have time to worsen.

Disease-related behaviors can create an avalanche of challenges for family caregivers. While there are times that medication is both necessary and appropriate, ideally it should not be the first line of defense. Most caregivers exercise great caution before considering any pharmacological interventions and the use of medications is frequently a topic at support group meetings. When in doubt, always have a discussion with the physician, consider alternatives, and focus on how to provide the best quality of life for your loved one.

Maintaining your emotional and physical health is also of the utmost importance. At one particular meeting years ago, the subject of caring for loved ones with agitation and anxiety was the hot topic. Naturally, this sparked numerous conversations and questions about some medications currently being prescribed by some of the area geriatric specialists, neurologists, and psychiatrists. Many pros and cons were expressed as was well as concerns about the potential side effects. One of the ladies brought up the name of a familiar antidepressant, and said since the doctor prescribed it, she had seen a big difference and, "My husband is not nearly as agitated as he had been." Another commented that she would be afraid to give that to her husband for fear it might make him drowsy and cause him to fall. "Oh no, I don't give that to my husband," the first lady said, "I take it. And now that I'm not so angry and irritated all the time, **his** moods have gotten so much better." There is a lot of truth and logic in that statement.

It's easy to forget that everything and everyone in their environment affects their dispositions, emotional responses, and behaviors. Caregivers play an enormous role in their personal surroundings. The popular saying, "If Mama ain't happy, ain't nobody happy," never rings truer than in a dementia care setting. Be it a family caregiver or a paid caregiver, that person's attitude and approach can set the tone for the entire day and play a vital role in assuring positive outcomes.

Some of my favorite and successful interventions for reducing or preventing agitation, anxiety or restlessness have been as simple as hugs, walks, and talks. A sense of calmness and pleasure can also come in the form of a cup of hot chocolate or herbal tea; hand, foot, back or head massage; or any enjoyable activities that are meaningful to them.

Music can also calm a restless soul. Many believe that listening to classical music for as little as twenty minutes a day will reduce agitation in those with Alzheimer's. It's referred to as the Mozart Effect. More recent research has shown the benefits of using personalized music to address these symptoms for those with Alzheimer's. Certainly, any or all of these are worth a try.

Before opting for sedative medications when sleeping is a problem, there are many other good suggestions for caregivers to try. Practice good sleep hygiene by encouraging loved ones go to bed and wake up around the same time each day. While it can be tempting for us to let loved ones sleep in for a few more hours in the morning for the additional peace and quiet, we often find it's not worth the tradeoff. When we're exhausted and wanting to sleep, we either struggle trying to get them into bed or end up with our loved ones wandering around the house throughout the wee hours of the morning.

Try enhancing nighttime sleep by offering milk at suppertime instead of iced tea, providing a bedtime snack, having a regular bedtime routine, spraying lavender on the pillow, linens or in the bedroom, or playing soothing music or nature sounds. Be sure that a trip to the toilet is always included in the nightly ritual.

Exercise is another good way to expel pent-up energy during the daytime to promote a good night's sleep, reduce agitation, and help prevent "sundowning syndrome." But be aware that too much physical activity is not always a good thing either. Develop daily routines to establish a balance between activities which are more physically active with ones more passive in nature. Alternate throughout the day so as to have calmer activities in and around mid-day. Liven-up the late afternoon by doing something more active to get the blood flowing, eject anxious bursts of liveliness, and overcome boredom. Keep in mind, what is good for the heart is good for the brain.

All of our bodies need time to rest and our brains need time to be restored. When our loved ones are consistently unable to achieve adequate amounts of restorative rest at night, we can allow time for a short nap, 30 minutes or less during the day and ideally only between the hours of 1:00 to 3:00. This allows ample time with a focus on napping not sleeping. Longer naps or too many will cause the person to become sleepier and groggier rather than feeling fresh and alert. Unless it is medically necessary or physically advisable, I strongly suggest beds be used only for nighttime "sleeping" and recliners or even a sofa be used for daytime "resting." As with almost everything else we do, it's about moderation.

Sleep issues need to be taken seriously as they can significantly affect both you and your loved one. Communicate your concerns and efforts with the doctor **before** the problem becomes completely unmanageable and someone's health and safety is in jeopardy. There might be other medical problems which should be addressed by a physician, such as sleep apnea, a common condition in older adults. In some situations, medication might be the only good option. Nighttime agitation and wandering can also cause sleep deprivation for caregivers, often prompting a family's decision for placement. Another option is to hire an experienced, bonded caregiver from an agency when nighttime issues create insurmountable problems while there is still a strong desire to keep a loved one at home for as long as possible and safely feasible.

With time and as we learn more, we become better caregivers. We're able to develop a different mindset, view everything with a renewed perspective, and willingly let go of what we cannot change. When a dear friend cared for his wife, he would often say, "IMP …It's my problem." It serves as a valuable reminder to caregivers, that we must be the ones to change. That's it. We recognize that anything they do or say that might annoy, disappoint, upset, or aggravate us is seldom a problem for our loved ones. More importantly we acknowledge, that even for us, these same things can only become a problem if we personally allow them to be a concern.

One thing we can always control is our response to a circumstance, remembering that frustration almost always sets in when we try to control something that is uncontrollable. An attitude of acceptance coupled with a changed perspective allows us to continue to move forward. We embrace each new day and focus on those good and special times, be it a few minutes, an hour, or a day. When we stumble across ways to make them laugh or smile, feel peace or calmness, we immerse ourselves in the enjoyment of each of these meaningful moments.

Every caregiver's day is filled with mind-over-matter situations. It is left up to us to decide what is most important — what truly matters. Each time we learn more, we are presented with yet another opportunity to do better. "Better" does not mean perfect. For a caregiver or any other person, it is a noble goal to begin each morning with a sincere intent to speak kindly, act lovingly, and serve gratefully.

When we know better, we realize that at the end of each day all that really, truly matters is love…kindness…respect… and acceptance.

> **"Each person's task in life is to become an increasingly better person."**
>
> **—Leo Tolstoy**

Acknowledgments

Did I Remember to Tell You? involved the efforts and support of many others and I am deeply indebted to each of them for their caring contributions. There are not words to fully express my heartfelt gratitude to all of these mentioned below, but "Thank You" seems a good place to start.

Since stories comprise the heart of the book, I want to first acknowledge and express my gratitude to the countless families that have shared their stories and encouraged me to include them in the book with the intent of helping others through this difficult journey. And my appreciation to Elaine Healy for permission to reprint her story in chapter 7.

Thank you to my dear friend Rose Romero and my wonderful mother-in-law, Betty Johnson, who read the first few chapters in the early days of the book, provided edits, comments, and sufficient encouragement for me to bravely move forward with this project.

I am grateful to my husband Mike Johnson. After several months and about 50 pages into the book, I felt that I simply did not have the necessary skills to write a book that would be any different than those currently available. It was my amazing and loving husband who encouraged me to start over and not give up. He persuaded me to find "my" voice and pursue the book with the same casual manner and enthusiasm as my workshops and presentations. He cheered me on and supported me throughout this entire endeavor.

A big thank you to my special friends Martha Taylor and Nancy

Rohm who spent months reading each chapter to confirm clarity, content, and correctness. They both provided helpful edits and comments. I also extend my gratitude to Martha for allowing me to reprint and share her heartwarming story about her mother in chapter 8. Additionally, I appreciate Nancy accepting hundreds of calls and texts from me for almost an entire year, asking for her opinions, thoughts, and suggestions.

My sincerest appreciation to Jerry McElveen for sharing his time and expertise to ensure correct grammar and punctuation. As an author, poet, and Professor of English Literature for Dallas County Community College District for over 40 years, I could not have had a more qualified editor or a better friend. His talents, skills and advice were invaluable, and I am incredibly grateful.

Most importantly, I am truly thankful to **God** for guiding my thoughts and words, bringing to mind these great stories, and allowing me to be of service to those living with Alzheimer's and their families.

About the Author

Pam Kovacs Johnson has spent most of her life working in long term care dedicated to meeting the needs of older adults and their families. During the past 45 years, her numerous professional positions in the field of aging have included Nursing Facility Administrator, Geriatric Care Manager, Director of Development for the Greater Dallas Chapter of the Alzheimer's Association, and dementia care consultant. In 2005, she founded Friends Place Adult Day Services, a specialized daytime program for individuals with short term memory problems, Alzheimer's, and other dementias.

Through the years, Pam has taught Alzheimer's and dementia caregiver classes and workshops, facilitated support groups, presented at care conferences, coordinated full day seminars for dementia family caregivers, and since 1984 has served in many volunteer capacities for the Alzheimer's Association.

In 2008, she became the primary caregiver for her father when he was diagnosed with Alzheimer's and vascular dementia. This personal experience coupled with her extensive professional knowledge and training prompted her to begin working on a guidebook for dementia family caregivers.

Now retired, she is devoting her time to empowering and educating dementia family caregivers through her writing, and at conferences, seminars, and community programs. As Pam prepares for her next book, When Is It Time, she welcomes any personal stories or comments which would help families that are trying to make difficult long-term care decisions.

Pam and her husband Mike live in Richardson, Texas, with their two "boys," dachshunds Toby and Tucker. They enjoy spending time with family and grandchildren, living locally and in the Phoenix area, and going to their cabin in the Ozarks near Eureka Springs, AR. She can be contacted at pamjohnson@Rockspire.com.